IDEAS & HOW-TO

Additions

SEP 2007

Meredith Books
Des Moines, Iowa

IDEAS & HOW-TO
Additions

Better Homes and Gardens® Ideas & How-To: Additions
Contributing Project Manager/Writer: Paul Krantz
Associate Design Director: Todd Emerson Hanson
Contributing Graphic Designer: David Jordan, Studio 22
Copy Chief: Terri Fredrickson
Copy Editor: Kevin Cox
Publishing Operations Manager: Karen Schirm
Senior Editor, Asset & Information Management: Phillip Morgan
Edit and Design Production Coordinator: Mary Lee Gavin
Editorial Assistant: Kaye Chabot
Book Production Managers: Pam Kvitne, Marjorie J. Schenkelberg,
   Rick von Holdt, Mark Weaver
Prepress Desktop Specialist: Ben Anderson
Contributing Copy Editor: Joyce Gemperlein
Contributing Proofreaders: Dan Degen, Pam Elizian, Heidi Johnson
Cover Photographer: Hedrich-Blessing Studio
Contributing Indexer: Sharon Duffy
Contributing Illustrators: Robert LaPointe, Larry Schlephorst

Meredith® Books
Executive Director, Editorial: Gregory H. Kayko
Executive Director, Design: Matt Strelecki
Managing Editor: Amy Tincher-Durik
Executive Editor: Benjamin W. Allen
Senior Editor/Group Manager: Vicki Leigh Ingham
Senior Associate Design Director: Ken Carlson
Marketing Product Manager: Brent Wiersma

Publisher and Editor in Chief: James D. Blume
Editorial Director: Linda Raglan Cunningham
Executive Director, Marketing: Kevin Kacere
Executive Director, New Business Development: Todd M. Davis
Executive Director, Sales: Ken Zagor

Director, Operations: George A. Susral
Director, Production: Douglas M. Johnston
Director, Marketing & Publicity: Amy Nichols
Business Director: Jim Leonard

Vice President and General Manager: Douglas J. Guendel

Better Homes and Gardens® **Magazine**
Editor in Chief: Gayle Goodson Butler
Deputy Editor, Home Design: Oma Blaise Ford

Meredith Publishing Group
President: Jack Griffin
Senior Vice President: Karla Jeffries

Meredith Corporation
Chairman of the Board: William T. Kerr
President and Chief Executive Officer: Stephen M. Lacy

In Memoriam: E.T. Meredith III (1933–2003)

All of us at Meredith® Books are dedicated to providing you with information and ideas to enhance your home. We welcome your comments and suggestions. Write to us at: Meredith Books, Home Decorating and Design Editorial Department, 1716 Locust St., Des Moines, IA 50309-3023.

Contents

4 PORCHES AND SUNROOMS

Welcome nature with a room that blends indoors and the great outdoors.

How-To and Advice:

5 ENTRY UPGRADES

Welcome guests with an entry that adds character to your home.

How-To and Advice:

6 TWO-STORY ADDITIONS

Take your plans to the next level with a multifunction add-on.

How-To and Advice:

7 MAKING IT HAPPEN

Tools, information, and advice for planning and building your addition.

Welcome

If you are considering adding onto your home, this idea-filled volume is a great place to start. Within these pages, you'll discover how people just like you have added on to create spacious kitchens, restful master suites, and flexible spaces for family gatherings and holiday entertaining. These examples, along with a trove of ideas and advice, will guide you as you plan and carry out your own projects.

4309

1 Kitchens and

A great kitchen is the soul of a home, a personal haven where you can reconnect with family and friends and enjoy the simple pleasures of food and conversation. In this chapter you'll find examples of kitchen and dining additions of all sizes. Though each is unique, all live up to the goal of creating an efficient workspace that also serves as the heart of the home.

See more of this addition on page 54.

Dining Spaces

■ Square Up a Corner

Small additions can set the stage for big improvements. Two modest additions—totaling fewer than 60 square feet—provided the elbow room needed to update this 1940s-era kitchen. To improve the traffic flow and create a sense of roominess, three existing areas (kitchen, laundry, and breakfast area) were combined into one flowing space. To improve storage, style, and functionality, an exterior corner of the kitchen was pushed out and a shallow bumpout was added to the adjacent wall (see the floor plans on page 12). These minor additions created the backdrop for a dramatic transformation.

The windows behind the desk mark the spot where the corner of the house was pushed out. To maintain the original character of the house, the addition includes a wraparound window like the one that graced the original kitchen. The chair shows the location of a small laundry room that was eliminated to make more room for the kitchen.

The star of the kitchen is a new island, which fits comfortably thanks to the added floor space. Its curved counter provides additional workspace and complements the archway above the compact home office, which nestles into a new 2-foot-deep bumpout. Built-in storage includes hanging file drawers and nearby cabinets for supplies.

In addition to keeping costs in check, choosing a modest kitchen add-on offers other benefits. A smaller addition usually sails more quickly through the permit process. Construction time is reduced too. This is particularly critical with a kitchen remodeling, which can be hard on a family that enjoys home-cooked meals on a regular basis.

The downside of thinking small is that it mandates careful planning. Details such as aisle clearances and storage needs take on much more importance when space is at a premium. Paradoxically that makes it more important to enlist the aid of an experienced kitchen designer for a small kitchen addition than for a large one.

This flip-up shelf is designed for base cabinets. The unit was installed adjacent to the prep sink to hold the food processor. An outlet inside the cabinet keeps electrical cords off the counter.

FLOOR PLANS ▧ addition area ▨ new structure

The floor plans illustrate the changes made to create the raw space for the new kitchen. Interior walls enclosing the laundry (which was relocated to the second floor) were torn out, and the two exterior walls were pushed out to square up the corner. The result was a flowing L-shape space that merges the kitchen and the breakfast area. The bumpout enabled the home office to be added without compromising the traffic flow around the island.

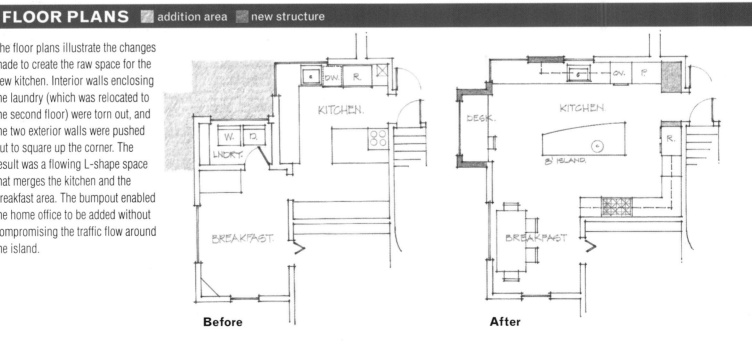

Before   After

The island serves as a full-featured work zone. A small refrigerator tucked into the end keeps drinks and breakfast foods within easy reach of children. Bread storage and a small prep sink make this a handy spot for fixing lunches and quick snacks. The oversize granite countertop makes a generous landing area for the wall ovens and the built-in refrigerator on the adjacent wall.

Small additions don't have to add up to cramped quarters. Here the bumpouts provided much of the room needed to lay out a good-size two-person kitchen. Key to the success of the new space is the island that anchors the three workstations—the sink, the cooktop, and the wall ovens. Stained a warm cherry and topped with the same granite as the counters, it's the focal point of the room.

The new cooktop is the heart of the active work zone. Pots and pans are within easy reach in a cabinet below the gas burners. Pullout vertical drawers located next to the cooktop provide quick access to spices, and drawers in the baseboard space store broiler pans. To the left a warming drawer keeps food at optimum temperature while last-minute preparations are completed.

Raised panels and simple brushed-nickel handles add interest to the wall of light-tone maple cabinets. Wide-plank flooring, accented with dark pegs, matches the home's original flooring. For a distinctive touch, the floor's overall finish is lighter.

The success of a kitchen often hinges on efficient storage. One goal of this remodeling project was to improve the quantity and quality of storage space. Ensuring that everything has a place helps achieve a sleek, uncluttered look, and the features shown on this page helped turn that concept into a reality.

Keeping staples corralled and organized is simple with the pantry closet next to the ovens. Narrow shelves on the door and rear wall ensure that nothing gets lost in the back row. A simple ceiling-mounted light illuminates the farthest corners of the unit.

Cubbies outfitted with doors and outlets keep small appliances out of sight when not needed. The doors slide up and out of the way under the wall cabinets.

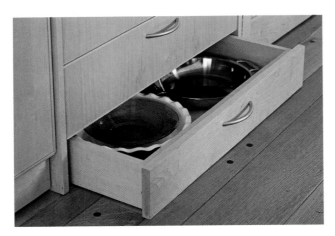

The toe-kick space under these cabinets is outfitted with drawers for storing bakeware that's used only occasionally. This narrow drawer also works for stashing pet food bowls when not in use.

Spices and herbs stay freshest in cool, dark storage. This pullout unit has slanted racks for easy access to frequently used items, plus plenty of space below for vinegars, oils, and condiments.

Today's best stock cabinets equal the quality found in custom units. Some off-the-shelf cabinet lines even sport features once limited to custom cabinets, such as toe-kick drawers. Here are some construction details to look for when shopping for new cabinets.

1. Side panels. ½- to ¾-inch plywood or medium-density fiberboard (MDF).

2. Back panel. ¼- to ⅜-inch plywood or MDF dado-joined to side panels.

3. Bracing. Corner blocks (or solid wood I-beams) at all corners.

4. Face frame (if used). ¾-inch solid wood assembled with doweled or mortise-and-tenon joints.

5. Shelves. ¾-inch plywood or MDF. Center supports for shelves more than 36 inches wide.

6. Glide-out accessories. Smooth, silent operation with three-quarters extension.

7. Doors. ¾-inch solid hardwood or veneered MDF. Laminate-faced doors should also be laminated on the back.

8. Hinges. Heavy-duty, fully adjustable.

9. Finish. Smooth, ripplefree, with satiny (not high-gloss) appearance. Woodgrain should match throughout. Interior materials and finish should be identical for open (doorless) cabinets.

10. Drawer boxes. ½- to ¾-inch solid wood or MDF full-height sides with dovetail joints. Plywood bottom set in dadoes (rectangular grooves in the drawer sides). Also acceptable are high-quality metal or thick plastic drawer boxes.

11. Drawer fronts. ¾-inch solid wood or MDF.

12. Drawer glides. Ball-bearing glides, 75-pound (or more) rating, three-quarters or more extension. Better units are self-closing.

■ Borrow Space to Improve a Floor Plan

Invest in a little extra space, then borrow the rest. This kitchen more than doubled in size even though only 48 square feet were added to the floor plan. The secret? The bulk of the "new space" came from incorporating an adjoining butler's pantry. This budget-savvy move improved the kitchen's traffic patterns and made room for a comfortable, well-equipped workspace.

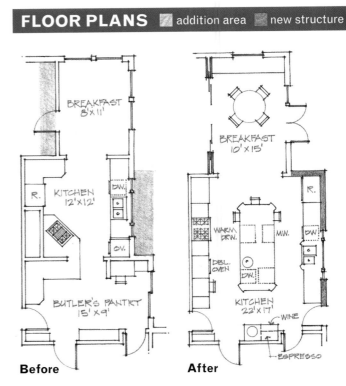

Adjacent to the kitchen, the breakfast room also benefited from a modest addition. An extra 2 feet of width creates clearance for the new French doors. Adding 4 feet at the rear further relieved the congestion and made room for a built-in buffet and storage units.

The original kitchen floor plan funneled traffic along the sink wall, causing inevitable congestion during cooking and cleanup. Another problem: The cooktop was uncomfortably close to the refrigerator. The new floor plan incorporates space from an old butler's pantry, providing better access to the kitchen from the other parts of the house. Although the new space is large, the arrangement is manageable because it is broken down into several work zones, each with its own storage and appliances. And all are served by the island, which easily holds prepared items and used utensils.

The 4×11-foot marble-top furniture-style island is outfitted to serve multiple work areas. In addition to bar seating, built-ins include a second dishwasher, a refrigerated drawer, a microwave, a warming drawer, and a small prep sink. The primary sink is centered in the wall that was pushed out 4 feet. Chandeliers over the island and the breakfast room table provide a visual connection between the two spaces.

Wide 48-inch aisles on two sides of the island provide plenty of room for traffic headed to the breakfast room.

The harlequin stone backsplash behind the range is an eyecatching detail and a practical touch. A custom ventilation hood matches the Hollywood-worthy drama of the overall design.

Sitting in space originally occupied by the butler's pantry, the beverage center serves admirably for entertaining. Features include a wet bar, a built-in espresso machine, and a wine refrigerator.

Borrowed space doesn't necessarily have to come from an adjacent room. In this home the kitchen gained an extra foot of width by incorporating space from a chase behind a range wall. (Chases, common in older homes, were designed to house items such as heating vents.) Other candidates for borrowing include stairwells, hallways, and closets. The feasibility of moving into these spaces hinges on being able to create a workable floor plan. But if borrowing is an option, you may be able to leverage a small addition into a larger kitchen.

HOW TO MAXIMIZE A KITCHEN ISLAND

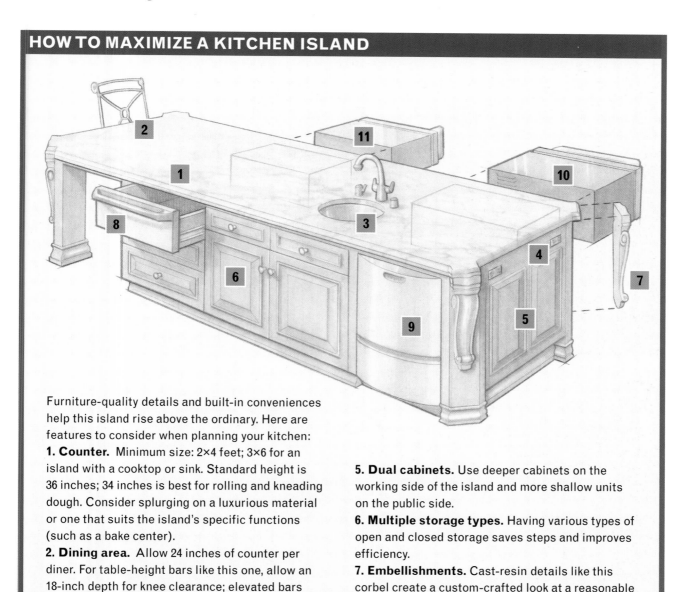

Furniture-quality details and built-in conveniences help this island rise above the ordinary. Here are features to consider when planning your kitchen:

1. Counter. Minimum size: 2×4 feet; 3×6 for an island with a cooktop or sink. Standard height is 36 inches; 34 inches is best for rolling and kneading dough. Consider splurging on a luxurious material or one that suits the island's specific functions (such as a bake center).

2. Dining area. Allow 24 inches of counter per diner. For table-height bars like this one, allow an 18-inch depth for knee clearance; elevated bars (typically 42 inches high) require only 12 inches.

3. Prep sink. Create a second work center with a small sink near the end of the island. Allow for an adjacent work surface and easy access to the refrigerator and utensils.

4. Outlets. For convenience and safety install an electrical outlet every 12 inches.

5. Dual cabinets. Use deeper cabinets on the working side of the island and more shallow units on the public side.

6. Multiple storage types. Having various types of open and closed storage saves steps and improves efficiency.

7. Embellishments. Cast-resin details like this corbel create a custom-crafted look at a reasonable price.

8. Convenience appliances. An island is the ideal location for a built-in warming drawer. Also worth considering: a second dishwasher **(9)** and a refrigerated drawer **(11)** near the prep sink and a microwave **(10)** that creates a secondary cook center.

■ Take Advantage of Patio Space

Link indoors and out to maximize an addition.
Before its renovation the kitchen in this 1788
Charleston, South Carolina, home barely measured
36 inches between the counters. Pushing out
one wall about 6 feet and another 2 feet relieved
congestion and created space for a small island/
breakfast bar. What really makes this small addition
shine are the new French doors leading to a tiny

backyard patio. Although neither the new kitchen
nor the patio are especially large, they add up to a
grand space.

**Even though it lost space to the addition, the 5×12-foot
patio is an integral part of the addition thanks to the French
doors. In addition to opening the two spaces to each other,
the doors and flanking windows funnel daylight deep into
the new kitchen.**

Originally the kitchen ended just to the right of the sink. During remodeling this wall was pushed out 2 feet. The 3×6-foot island replaces a section of counter that formed one leg of the U-shape layout. Set 2 inches lower than the usual 36-inch counter height, the island's honed Venetino marble top is at the ideal level for working bread dough.

Blending a small addition with a patio, deck, or porch can maximize your remodeling budget. Although it is most effective in temperate climates, this approach can work elsewhere too. In the cold north choose a southern exposure protected from cold winds. In the far south seek the shade of a north-facing wall. Heating and cooling units rated for outdoor use can extend the seasons even more.

Though modest in size, the island sports convenience features including a dining bar, cookbook storage, and a microwave. Crafted detailing harks back to the past, when kitchens were fitted with furniture instead of built-ins.

The desk marks the location of the 5×12-foot added space. The casing around the window was milled to match woodwork elsewhere in the house. Salvaged from the home's upper level, the heart pine flooring was remilled before installation.

Load-bearing walls in older homes are often quite thick, illustrated here by the opening between the addition and the dining room. Paneling turns this awkward detail into an elegant passageway.

FLOOR PLANS addition area new structure

Rather than contend with an aging structure, the old kitchen was torn down, but the new space was crafted to match the proportions of the original. A major benefit of the added space is an improved traffic flow from dining room to patio. Reconfiguring the half bath turned this enclosed space into a wide hallway with direct access to the kitchen.

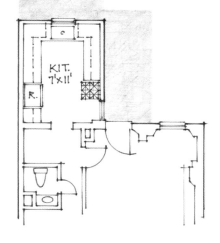

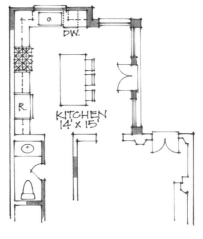

Before

After

To make the new space feel larger, the original 12-foot ceiling height was maintained. A creamy color scheme, a brick-laid tile backsplash, paneled cabinetry, and honey-tone flooring create a look that's appropriate to an 18th-century home.

Expand with a Breakfast Room

Using diagonal sight lines creates interest. Artists and designers know that the human eye is attracted to lines that run outside the box. In this kitchen/breakfast room addition, a diagonal relationship between the two spaces sparks plenty of visual appeal. The two rooms run across the rear of the 1915 Italianate house, but the 16×22-foot kitchen projects 10 feet farther back. The result: Views from one room to the other are controlled, even though they are joined by an 8-foot-wide archway.

Although mostly open to the kitchen, the new breakfast room maintains its own character. The beaded-board wall treatment used in the kitchen gives way to tall, paneled wainscoting here. Antique furnishings and a ruddy-tone area rug offer a warm contrast to the cooler colors of the kitchen.

Glass-front cabinets combine storage and display around the sink. Other custom touches, such as the stack of small drawers, provide visual interest as well as convenient storage for smaller items such as dish towels, coffee filters, and plastic bags.

The diagonal sight line from breakfast room to kitchen adds visual interest. As you move farther back into the breakfast room, the view of the sink area—potentially the messiest in a kitchen—is blocked. The island, with its white granite countertop, turned legs, and bentwood apron, provides a focal point for this view.

A small home office sits in an alcove adjacent to the kitchen, ensuring that clutter on the desk stays out of sight. Access to a walk-in pantry is through this space.

The prep center is outfitted with versatile storage and a mixing counter flanked by a refrigerator and matching freezer; a small prep sink is in the island. The six-burner commercial-style range provides cooking power for everything from family dinners to grand entertaining.

FLOOR PLAN new structure

One benefit of the diagonal arrangement of the new rooms is excellent traffic flow. Aisles and doorways are placed so that pathways tend toward the sides and corners of the spaces, rather than through the middle of them. Designing traffic flow can be a real challenge, especially in older homes that have multiple access points to each room.

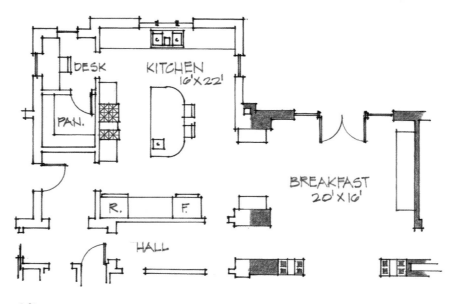

DESK

KITCHEN
16' X 22'

PAN.

R.   F.

BREAKFAST
20' X 16'

HALL

After

The major downside of a diagonal arrangement of rooms is that you may need to add an "inside corner" to the addition's exterior wall. As builders will quickly explain, each extra corner adds to the cost of an addition. But if the budget numbers work, you'll find that breaking out of the box mentality can add a measure of interest to your home.

HOW TO OUTFIT A PREP CENTER

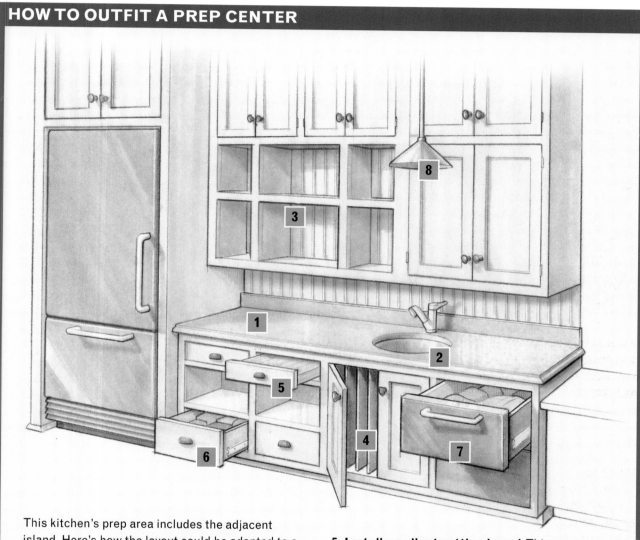

This kitchen's prep area includes the adjacent island. Here's how the layout could be adapted to a kitchen without an island:

1. Lengthen the counter. Choose a functional material such as marble for rolling pastry or stain-resistant solid-surfacing for prep work. Allow at least 3 feet of clear counterspace, more if possible.

2. Incorporate a prep sink. Essential for prep areas; desirable for baking centers.

3. Add accessible storage. Provide open storage for frequently used items such as paper or cloth towels, knives, and cookbooks.

4. Add specialized storage. Make provisions for awkward items such as cookie sheets, as well as storage tailored to spices, flour, and sugar.

5. Install a pullout cutting board. This saves space and is always handy.

6. Include produce bins. Deep, ventilated drawers can provide cool, dark storage for items such as potatoes or onions or space for packaged items.

7. Build in extra refrigerated storage. If you entertain frequently and your budget can handle it, consider installing one or two refrigerated drawers to reduce steps and provide extra holding space. For a less expensive option, install an undercounter refrigerator.

8. Brighten with task lighting. Use pendent or undercabinet fixtures to create shadow-free counters.

■ Open Up the Kitchen

Bridge old spaces with new to unify rooms. That approach was used to meet the goal of this great-room kitchen addition, which can accommodate parties for up to 36 people. The key to making it work was an addition that allowed a new kitchen to join forces with an existing sunroom. The result is a single flowing space that includes a five-sided island with plenty of seating, a small breakfast area, and a sunken seating area for lively conversation.

It's hard to tell where the old sunroom ends and the new 10×12-foot addition begins because a new gable roof unifies the combined spaces. To blend new and old, some of the tall, transom-topped windows originally in the sunroom were transplanted to the addition.

Although new and old blend beautifully here, there is one visible reminder of the changes: the difference in ceiling height between the original sunroom and the newly added space. Extending the sunroom's vaulted ceiling into the new space would have entailed rebuilding the entire roof and ceiling structure. Instead, the original gabled roof supports were left in place, and a new roof with similar slope was extended over the addition.

Blending the old and new in this project required some fancy footwork. That's because the sunroom was built one step lower than the rest of the house. The solution was to extend the step around the entire perimeter of the seating area so guests could wander more freely throughout the great-room. Aligning the tops of the windows keeps the change in level from calling too much attention to itself.

One principle guiding the remodeling was "you can never have too many windows." That led to the novel idea of nixing the usual tile backsplash behind the sink in favor of a pair of windows that open out awning-style.

FLOOR PLANS ▨ addition area ▨ new structure

Because of the quality of the original sunroom construction, filling in the open space was a relatively simple process. To garner more space for the kitchen, the old one was gutted and the original exterior wall removed. Only minor changes to the interior walls were needed, and the original link between the kitchen and family room was maintained.

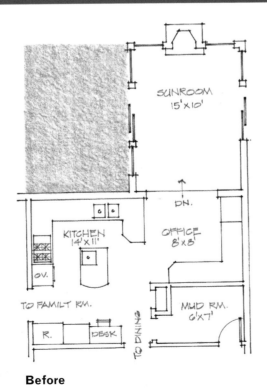

Before

SUNROOM
15' x 10'

DN.

KITCHEN
14' x 11'

OFFICE
8' x 8'

OV.

TO FAMILY RM.

R.   DESK

TO DINING

MUD RM.
6' x 7'

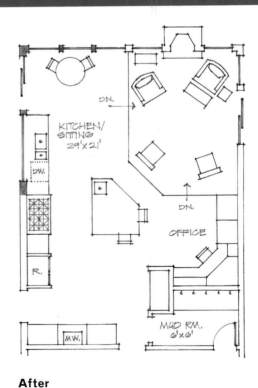

After

DN.

KITCHEN/
SITTING
29' x 21'

DW.

DN.

OFFICE

R.

M.W.

MUD RM.
6' x 6'

The change in floor and ceiling levels gives the great-room a subtle feeling of separation from the adjacent kitchen and office while preserving the open, airy character of the space. A large rug anchors the seating area visually and helps create welcoming warmth.

Blending old and new flooring can be difficult, especially if the original is worn. New wide-plank oak flooring extends throughout the remodeled area, enhancing the light-filled quality of the space.

There's no law that utilitarian tools have to be dull, as the island's vegetable sink proves. Inspired by Italian Renaissance ceramics, the sink also guided the great-room's color palette.

Design elements give the room a unified look when one large space must serve several functions. The repetition of the tall windows, whose small panes are echoed in the glass-front cabinets, serves just such a unifying purpose. But even the details in this great-room serve that goal. For example, the blues, yellows, and greens in the island's distinctive prep sink influenced the color scheme used throughout the space. Indeed, decor, as much as architectural design, can be a potent tool for blending new and old spaces.

HOW TO INSTALL A TILE COUNTERTOP

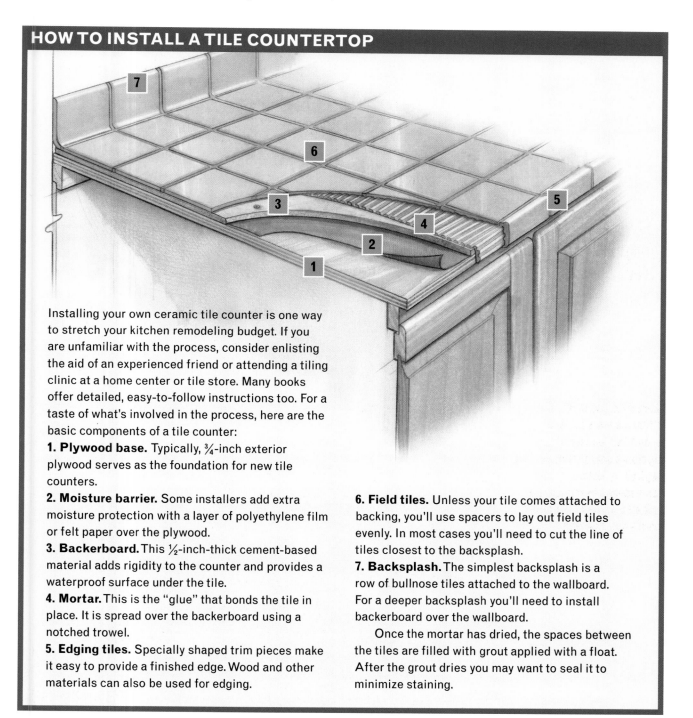

Installing your own ceramic tile counter is one way to stretch your kitchen remodeling budget. If you are unfamiliar with the process, consider enlisting the aid of an experienced friend or attending a tiling clinic at a home center or tile store. Many books offer detailed, easy-to-follow instructions too. For a taste of what's involved in the process, here are the basic components of a tile counter:

1. Plywood base. Typically, ¾-inch exterior plywood serves as the foundation for new tile counters.

2. Moisture barrier. Some installers add extra moisture protection with a layer of polyethylene film or felt paper over the plywood.

3. Backerboard. This ½-inch-thick cement-based material adds rigidity to the counter and provides a waterproof surface under the tile.

4. Mortar. This is the "glue" that bonds the tile in place. It is spread over the backerboard using a notched trowel.

5. Edging tiles. Specially shaped trim pieces make it easy to provide a finished edge. Wood and other materials can also be used for edging.

6. Field tiles. Unless your tile comes attached to backing, you'll use spacers to lay out field tiles evenly. In most cases you'll need to cut the line of tiles closest to the backsplash.

7. Backsplash. The simplest backsplash is a row of bullnose tiles attached to the wallboard. For a deeper backsplash you'll need to install backerboard over the wallboard.

Once the mortar has dried, the spaces between the tiles are filled with grout applied with a float. After the grout dries you may want to seal it to minimize staining.

■ Add Farmhouse Style

Before you start planning, try this: Kitchen planners often suggest starting with a wish list to help focus your remodeling plans. The kitchen on these pages, however, grew out of a "don't want" list: no snack counter, no television, and no "eat and run" mentality. Instead, the kitchen is designed to encourage family time, with a real dining table where parents and kids can sit down and enjoy a meal together without distractions. If you understand both your likes *and* dislikes, you'll be better positioned to achieve a satisfying—and affordable—result with your remodeling project.

Though not part of the original plan, a kitchen alcove was added to accommodate a farmhouse-style table and walnut bench. The table's generous dimensions make it perfect for homework and craft projects as well as daily family meals.

The kitchen's 4×7-foot worktable includes a marble surface that's ideal for rolling out pizza dough or making grandma's peanut brittle. It's big enough to allow several family members to use it at the same time.

The farmhouse sink, with its single deep bowl and wallmount faucet, is ideal for jobs such as creating flower arrangements and washing family-size roasting pans.

With its prep sink, toaster, and coffeemaking supplies, the breakfast station adjacent to the kitchen table offers an efficient start to the day.

FLOOR PLANS ▨ addition area ▨ new structure

The new kitchen is part of an extensive two-story add-on. The original butler's pantry off the dining room was retained, and another small pantry was added adjacent to the kitchen. (This is the location of the family's seldom-used microwave.)

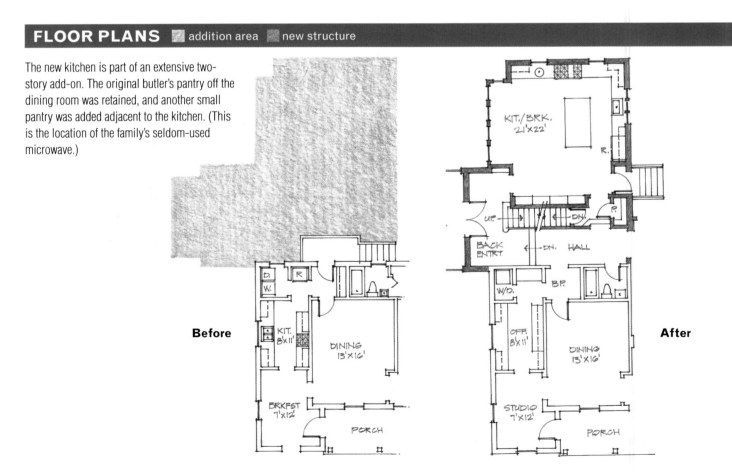

Before

After

The easiest way to build your "don't want" list is to keep a diary of what annoys you about your current home. For example, you may bristle when guests wander into the kitchen while you are cooking. Or perhaps you don't like the noise and humidity generated by the laundry next to your bedroom. Having your pet peeves on paper can help you resist the advice offered by experts who say that every kitchen should be designed for entertaining and every home needs an upper-level laundry.

Although you'd never know it from the front, the addition includes the new rear entry and everything to its left. Matching brick siding, rooflines, and general proportions allow the old and new sections to coexist peacefully.

Measuring 11 feet long and 18 inches deep, the built-in floor-to-ceiling china press stores as much as a good-size pantry, with the added bonus of display space. Custom drawers and shelves accommodate everything from daily dinnerware to oversize serving pieces and folded napkins.

■ Bump Out with a Bay

Little add-ons can enhance a bigger project.
This charming dinette is just one small part of the much larger addition shown on pages 86–89. It's a 2×7-foot box bay window set into the endwall of a kitchen. Outfitted with a 48-inch round table, a few chairs, and the bay's own window seat, it's the perfect place to grab a cup of coffee in the morning or to enjoy the paper over an afternoon snack.

Bays are a cost-effective way to add square footage. Most are less than 48 inches deep and often do not require a foundation. Depending on the width of the bay, only relatively simple reinforcements are needed to support the new opening in the exterior wall. Installing a window seat eliminates the need to match the flooring.

Touches such as a mini chandelier and curlicue brackets add character and help make the nook feel special. Look for brackets similar to these at architectural salvage firms or buy new ones at a home center and give them a faux-aged paint treatment.

HOW A BUMPOUT WORKS

Because it doesn't require a new foundation, a bumpout is a budget-friendly way to add on. Whether just large enough for a bay window or running the entire length of a wall, a bumpout is generally limited to a depth of 4 feet; most bumpouts extend about 2 feet from the foundation. The two diagrams show typical floor framing for two common situations.

1. When the joists run parallel to the foundation wall, sections of several existing joists are removed, and the bumpout's joists are attached to the first uncut joist.

2. If the existing joists run perpendicular to the foundation, the bumpout's joists are nailed to their sides, a technique called sistering.

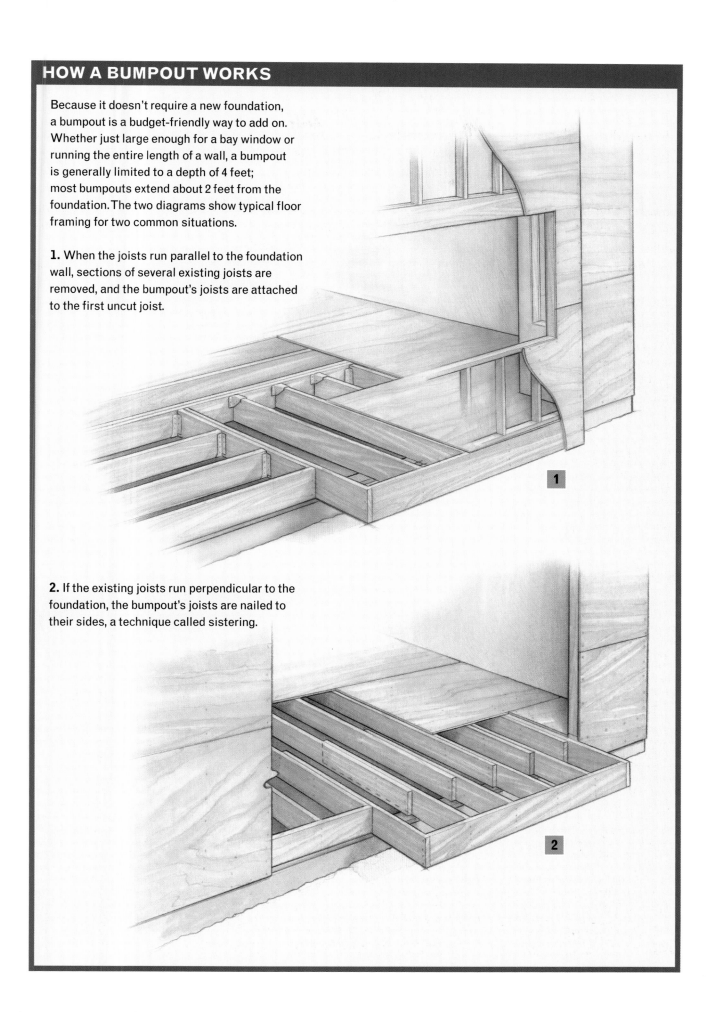

■ Gain Space with a Built-In Bench

Banquettes are perfect for breakfast areas. If you're adding an eating area to your kitchen, consider the spacesaving benefits of including a banquette as well—a comfortable bench built into a wall. The one shown here wraps around two sides of a 5½×10-foot addition and seats five comfortably. The addition was part of a larger overhaul of an outdated kitchen (see the floor plans on page 44) and solved another major problem: too little daylight. Wrapped in windows chosen to match those in the rest of the house, the new breakfast area overlooks the patio and garden.

The shed-roofed add-on that houses the breakfast area is proportioned to look like a part of the original house. Extending the roof over the entry created the covered front porch that now greets visitors. The impetus for the addition was the remodeling of the home's outdated kitchen.

Roman shades provide low-profile window coverage when needed but fold discretely out of the way during the day so the view can take center stage. An inexpensive rug helps define the seating area.

The new kitchen gained just enough width to allow an island, which dramatically boosts storage and counterspace. The island's prep sink and built-in microwave permit two cooks to coexist comfortably. A half-wall behind the farmhouse sink provides a view to the backyard.

Built-in cabinets adjacent to the breakfast area offer floor-to-ceiling storage and a rotating pullout shelf for the TV. Similar shallow built-ins line one wall of the kitchen.

FLOOR PLANS ▨ addition area ▨ new structure

Adding the dining nook meant stealing space from the old kitchen. To make up for the loss, the stairway in the main entry was reconfigured to allow a hallway to be eliminated. The kitchen wall moved into the hallway's place, and a half bath was eliminated. The dining bumpout also improved traffic flow and created room for a secondary entrance.

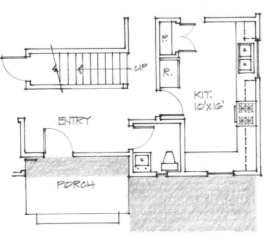

Before

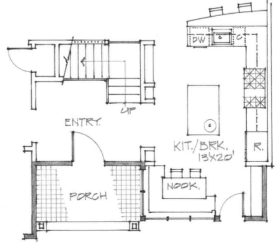

After

A banquette provides dining space in less square footage than a typical table-and-chairs arrangement. Unlike the fixed confines of a booth, a banquette can be fitted with tables of different sizes, depending on the size of the crowd—or no table at all for just plain lounging. These versatile benches also can provide underseat storage, an important efficiency when you consider the cost of adding space to your home.

HOW TO DESIGN A BANQUETTE

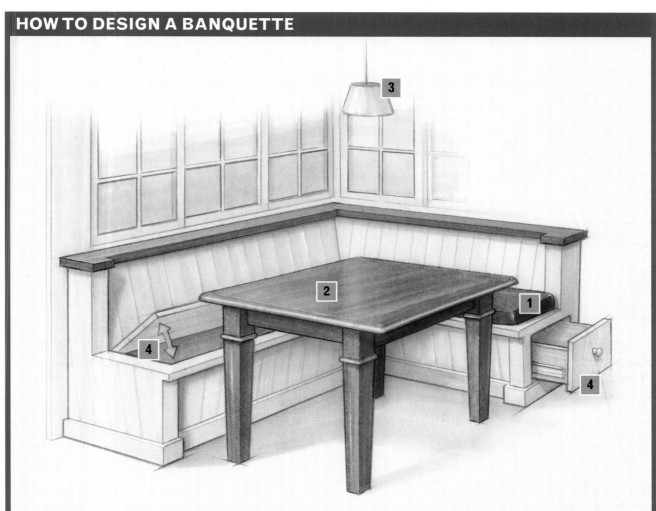

A banquette is an upholstered bench, ideally with cushion seats and a slightly reclining back. When installed against a wall and equipped with a table, it provides space-efficient seating for dining or working. To use chairs on the outer edges of the table, allow at least 44 inches of clearance between the table edge and a wall or traffic path. Design features to consider:

1. Benches. Typically built into the wall, they also may be freestanding. To maximize space, wrap them around a corner. Seat height should be 16 to 18 inches with about 12 inches of clearance between seat level and the underside of the table. Seat depth is 16 inches.

2. Table. Allow at least 21 inches of table space per person. For two-sided dining with chairs on the outside, the table should be at least 30 inches across.

3. Lighting. A pendent fixture with a dimmer switch provides illumination and mood control. Use a 150-watt incandescent bulb (or equivalent). If the banquette is next to a window, provide shades or draperies for light control and privacy.

4. Storage. If you are custom-building a banquette, consider adding storage under the seats for infrequently used items such as holiday linens. Hinged bench seats are easiest to install, but drawers provide faster access.

▪ Wrap a Corner to Add Space

A small addition can rescue a floor plan. One of the problems with eat-in kitchens is that the table typically sits in the only clear floor space, where it interferes with traffic. This sunny dining nook solves that problem by being tucked into a small addition that wraps the corner of the house. The three-sided banquette seats four, with another two places available on the outside of the table—all this without blocking the aisle.

The bumpout, which wraps a front corner of the house, matches the rest of the 1925 Mediterranean-influenced exterior. Stucco siding and divided-pane windows, proportioned to match the windows on the front of the house, ensure a seamless blend.

Windows on three sides of the bumpout funnel plenty of light into the new kitchen and provide a panoramic view of the home's landscaped surroundings. Storage drawers underneath the benches reduce the need for wall cabinets in the main kitchen area.

The island's Carrara marble work surface and prep sink ease the job of the chef. Across the way the cleanup area offers a step-saving arrangement of double-bowl sink, dishwasher, and plenty of storage. Along the back wall of the entry, a pantry with glass doors serves as storage and display case.

FLOOR PLANS addition area new structure

The new floor plan provides many more direct routes between the kitchen and other parts of the house. Incorporating the old back hallway into the kitchen preserves its use as a traffic lane and provides extra space around the end of the island.

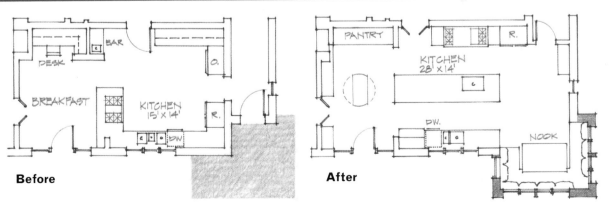

Before

After

In the home's original layout, the front entry led directly into a breakfast area next to the kitchen. Adding the dining nook relieved the entry of its double-duty status, though a small table remains. The reconfigured kitchen layout provides a pair of work zones that share the central island. Because the nook keeps diners out of the aisles, traffic can flow smoothly around either side of the island, which is not a bad payoff for such a modest investment in new space.

HOW TO PLUMB AN ISLAND SINK

Kitchen plumbing involves two systems, one that supplies water and one that provides drainage and venting. The vent pipes permit gases to escape and allow the air flow necessary for drainpipes to function properly. A vent pipe needs to extend at least 6 inches above the top of the fixture. Because that's not possible when a sink is installed in an island, the plumber usually creates a U-shape arrangement of drainpipes, with the top of the U as high as possible. Both sides of the U connect to the drainpipe; one side of the U connects to the vent system in a nearby wall **(1)**.

A simpler alternative is to install an "air admittance valve" instead of the U. Although this eliminates the need to connect to the home's vent system, the setup doesn't drain as effectively, so some plumbers and local building officials are reluctant to endorse them. Proceed with caution especially if you plan to install a dishwasher in the island.

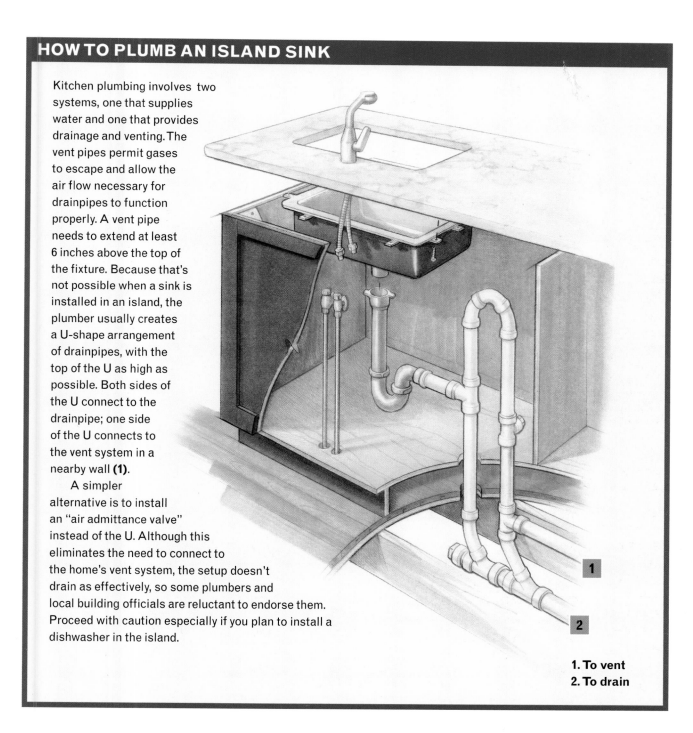

1. To vent
2. To drain

■ Improve Flow and Function

A dining addition makes the kitchen fun. Almost any size kitchen can become schmooze-central if it offers a generous eating area. Good food—coupled with a design that allows guests to mix it up with the hosts/chefs—is all it takes to launch a lively party. In this home a 150-square-foot dining addition transformed a dreary kitchen into an entertainment powerhouse. The new 16×10-foot eating area borrowed space from the old kitchen and matches the size of the revamped one; both areas are designed to foster an air of camaraderie throughout the space.

Set into the kitchen's island, the range offers a commanding view of the dinette area. The down-vented range, combined with the wide counter, keeps guests a comfortable distance from cooking fumes and spatters. A compact work triangle makes it easy for the chef to stay in the conversation.

The swoopy curves of the table set a fun and convivial tone for the new dinette tucked into a dramatic 20-foot-tall addition. A long, wraparound banquette encourages interaction among diners. And because the seating squarely faces the kitchen, there's no craning your neck to talk

To complete the transition from kitchen to entertainment center, just add stunning decor. In this case a mix of stainless steel, warm-tone wood, and a black and white color palette provides an appealing setting for the show. Mood lighting is also helpful for establishing a sophisticated feeling, and a beverage center helps keep guests' glasses filled. Even without these pleasantries you'd still have a great place for entertaining, thanks to the generous dining add-on.

Shelves behind one end of the banquette provide convenient cookbook storage and display space for objects that personalize the room.

FLOOR PLANS ▨ addition area ▨ new structure

Floor space added during the remodeling wasn't used to increase the size of the kitchen itself. The added space improved traffic flow with wide aisles and generous clearances. As the plans illustrate, the island helps route traffic around the work core rather than through it. The island's size also makes it ideal for a buffet setup.

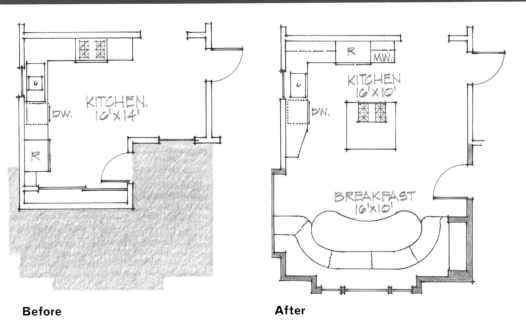

KITCHEN.
16'x14'

DW.

R

Before

R   MW.

KITCHEN
16'x10'

DW.

BREAKFAST
16'x10'

After

Though small, the kitchen doesn't lack for one amenity that's an integral part of almost any entertaining area: a bar. Tucked conveniently between refrigerator and sink, the beverage preparation area keeps plenty of glassware on display and close at hand.

Expand with Space and Light

A well-planned addition adds more than square footage. It can also add daylight. Dark and dismal, the original kitchen in this home suffered from its position just inside the porch. Down went the porch, and in its place arose a sunny breakfast room. An archway flanked by columns defines the line between the dining and kitchen spaces but allows light and conversation to flow freely. Now light streams unimpeded through the space and into the updated kitchen.

The add-on includes a large deck with access to the breakfast room and the kitchen. Daylight reaches the kitchen via both routes. The small window on the right brightens a half bath, which was moved from its previous location in the kitchen.

FLOOR PLANS   addition area   new structure

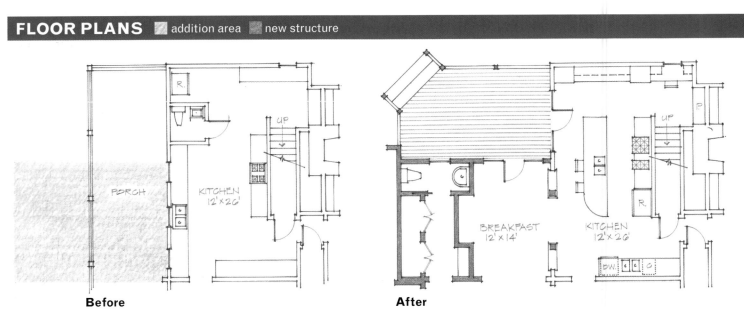

Before

After

The original layout of the kitchen was a mess, with a half bath blocking easy access to the refrigerator. Moving the bath to the addition made room for the island, reducing the size of the work triangle. In the original layout the distance from sink to refrigerator to stove was 34 feet, far longer than the traditional suggested limit of 21 feet. A new planning desk is tucked under a window near the stairs.

The large opening between the dining addition and kitchen required shoring up because it sits within a wall that supports the home's second floor. Although they look decorative, the columns flanking the opening provide structural support. Without the columns the beam above the opening would be larger, reducing the height of the opening.

The kitchen's amber-tone maple cabinetry extends from baseboard to ceiling, providing plenty of storage despite the lack of wall cabinets between the kitchen and eating area. The original floor, still in place, is also maple. Front and center, the island serves as home for the primary sink, as well as a wraparound breakfast bar. The soapstone countertop adds a rich contrast to the lighter tones that predominate.

At the far end of the kitchen, a full-size sink, dishwasher, and microwave provide a work zone for a second cook. Brick-patterned backsplashes here and behind the range provide visual relief from the large expanse of wood.

Light flows as easily as water, provided obstructions are removed. In the case of this kitchen, that meant trading out a wall of base and wall cabinets for an island. Keeping the color palette warm and bright also helps. Other options for bringing light into a space include skylights, clerestory windows (located high on a wall), and light tubes, which are highly reflective hollow columns that channel light from a clear dome mounted outside the house. Although excessive sunlight can fade fabrics, modern window coatings can block the active UV rays to protect interiors.

HOW TO VENT A COOKTOP

A properly sized vent system exhausts damaging cooking fumes and moisture to the outside. The canopy area should at least equal that of the range top, and the capacity should be at least 150 cubic feet per minute (CFM); commercial-style ranges require much more powerful systems. Follow local codes and manufacturer instructions when selecting and installing a vent system. If there is attic space above the range, running the ductwork through the roof is an option. The illustrations show some common installation options where roof venting is not feasible.

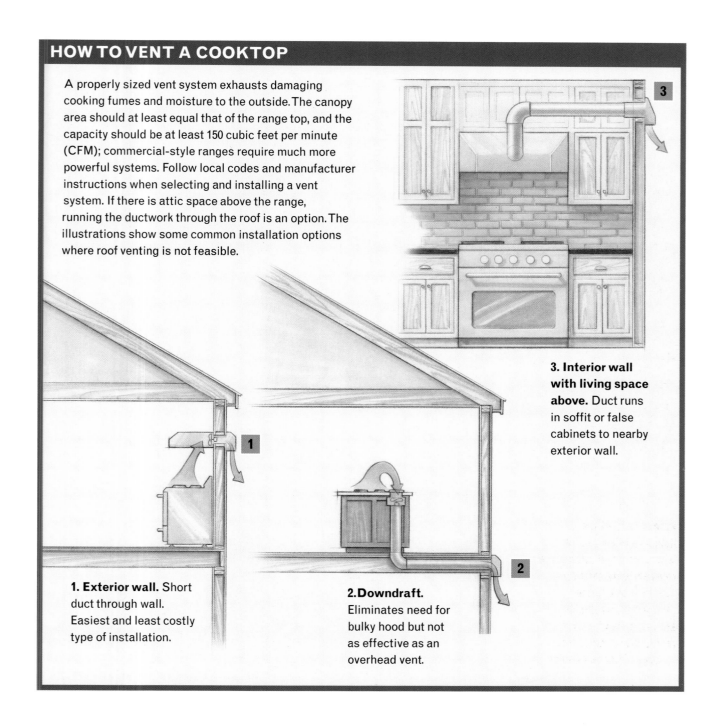

3. Interior wall with living space above. Duct runs in soffit or false cabinets to nearby exterior wall.

1. Exterior wall. Short duct through wall. Easiest and least costly type of installation.

2. Downdraft. Eliminates need for bulky hood but not as effective as an overhead vent.

■ Subtract Before Adding

With older homes, consider undoing before redoing. That's what happened to this 1895 Queen Anne Victorian. Before the remodeling a small, out-of-character addition provided the home's only dining space. Removing that section of the house made way for a dramatic transformation.

A new 13×10-foot dining addition arose at the original outside wall of the old breakfast room. On the exterior the new and old structures were blended with a skillful match of materials and details.

The brickwork and rough-cut stone sills under the addition's windows match those on the main house. The scalloped siding matches the siding on the dormer. Even the brackets under the roof overhang echo those on the existing structure. Attention to details like this can be expensive, but it helps maintain value, particularly in a historic home.

Trimwork around the windows, hardwood flooring, and wide crown molding at the ceiling reflect the style of craftsmanship in the original structure. A set of French doors provides access to the brick patio and garden.

Sliding the kitchen into the old breakfast room opened a space at the back of the kitchen. This area, closed off with a new partial wall, was transformed into a small mudroom, complete with a farmhouse sink and pullout sprayer for big cleaning jobs.

FLOOR PLANS ▧ addition area ▨ new structure

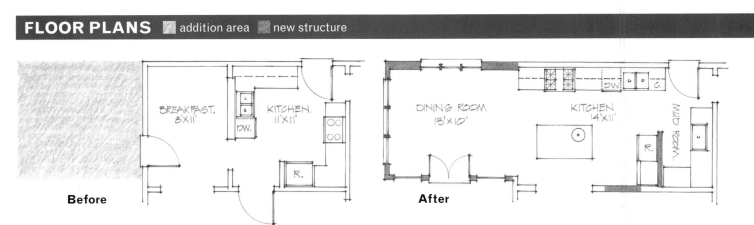

Before

BREAKFAST. 8'X11'

KITCHEN. 11'X11'

DW.

R.

After

DINING ROOM 13'X10'

KITCHEN 14'X11'

DW.

MUD ROOM

R.

The before and after plans illustrate the dramatic improvement of traffic flow resulting from the changes. The work triangle is now compact and doesn't require crossing the entire kitchen. The new mudroom means that people coming in from the yard no longer enter directly into the kitchen.

Making the decision to remove a portion of a house is rarely easy. But it can be a reasonable move, particularly if the section slated for removal is damaged, defective, or out of character with the rest of the house. With luck the old foundation can be used to support some or all of the addition; however, it is critical to confer with a structural engineer before assuming the old foundation is capable of supporting new construction.

The remodeled kitchen was enlarged and moved partially into the former breakfast room. The jog in the wall cabinets to the right of the range marks the original outer wall of the kitchen. Removing that wall revealed patchwork in the original brick wall, a slight imperfection that adds character.

Planning Guide for Kitchens

CHOOSING A KITCHEN LAYOUT

A good way to start planning a kitchen addition is to select the layout that best meets your needs. Use the descriptions below to explore the options. Bear in mind that any layout can be made larger, but that the work triangle—the path from sink to cooktop to refrigerator—should total between 12 and 26 feet and that each leg of the triangle should measure between 4 and 9 feet in length.

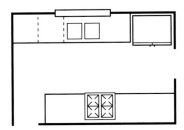

Two-Wall Galley
Best For: Limited spaces, limited construction budget, basic work centers, one cook, privacy
Tips: Allow at least 48 inches between counters to keep appliance doors from interfering with traffic flow.

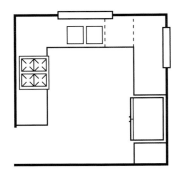

U-Shape
Best For: Small to average-size spaces, basic work centers, one cook
Tips: Allow a minimum of 60 inches between the legs of the U; 72 inches is preferred.

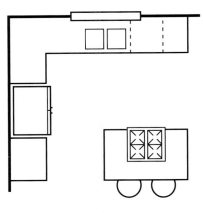

L with Island
Best For: Average-size to large spaces, basic plus specialty work centers, multiple cooks
Tips: Islands work best in a space at least 10×10 feet and open to another room. Walkways should be at least 36 inches wide; allow 42 inches for work aisles.

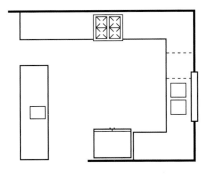

Two-Cook
Best For: Large spaces, basic plus specialty work centers, multiple cooks
Tips: Twin work triangles allow two cooks to work with maximum comfort. The large island allows installation of a second sink or cooktop plus a small refrigerator.

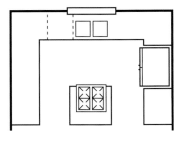

U with Island
Best For: Average-size to large spaces, basic plus specialty work centers, multiple cooks
Tips: Avoid situations where the island blocks the path between primary work centers. Place specialty work centers, such as a prep area, outside the primary work triangle.

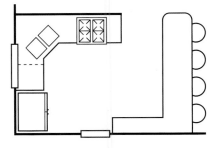

L with Peninsula
Best For: Large spaces, entertaining or casual dining
Tips: Adding a cooktop or prep sink to the peninsula turns this into a workable multicook kitchen.

NUMBERS TO KNOW

Before you finalize your kitchen plan, check to see that it measures up to the recommendations of top kitchen designers.

	Recommended Minimums	Tips
Aisles and Doorways	42-inch-wide walkways; 48 inches for work aisles; 32 inches of clear opening for doorways	For two-cook kitchens aisle should be at least 48 inches wide. Door swings should not interfere with appliances.
Sink	Landing areas of 24 inches on one side, 18 inches on the other	Install dishwasher within 36 inches of sink; door should not block sink when open.
Refrigerator	15-inch landing area on handle side (either side for side-by-side model)	Alternative landing location: on an island no more than 48 inches away
Cooktop/Range	12-inch landing zone on one side; 15 inches on the other side	For island installations allow at least 9 inches behind cooking surface. Note: Follow all manufacturer specifications.
Microwave	Bottom of oven 36 to 54 inches from floor; 15-inch-wide landing area adjacent	Undercounter microwaves should be at least 15 inches above the floor.
Oven	15-inch-wide landing area above or beside oven	Alternative location for landing area: on an island no more than 48 inches away.
Storage/Counters	16 lineal feet of base cabinets; 14 lineal feet of wall cabinets; 12 lineal feet of countertop	For kitchens less than 150 square feet in size, allow 13 feet of base cabinets, 12 feet of wall cabinets, and 11 feet of countertops.

ACCESSIBLE KITCHEN DESIGN

The principles of universal design make life easier for everyone, not just those who use wheelchairs. The recommendations below are designed with wheelchair access in mind. For more information about using universal design throughout your home, see page 213.

Clearances. Doorways and aisles should be at least 34 inches wide. Remember to factor in door frames and appliance handles when measuring. A standard wheelchair requires a 5-foot circle for turning.

Counters. Maximum height 34 inches; maximum depth 21 inches. At sink, cooktop, and food prep areas, allow a knee space that is at least 27 inches tall, 30 inches wide, and 19 inches deep.

Sink Area. A shallow sink (8-inch depth) and single-handle control. Drains should be arranged not to interfere with knee space.

Cooktop/Oven. A separate cooktop with knee space below is ideal. Controls should be in front and the burners staggered to avoid the need to reach over them. Wallmount ovens should be installed at an accessible height. There should

be at least 15 inches of accessible countertop on one side of a cooking appliance.

Storage. Make base cabinet storage accessible by using turntables in corner units and pullout trays in other cabinets.

Outlets and Switches. Electrical outlets should be at least 15 inches above floor level. Light switches should be no more than 48 inches above floor level.

Planning Guide for Kitchens

COUNTERTOPS FOR THE LONG RUN

Some countertop materials, such as marble and wood, are very expensive or best suited to specialized work areas. The materials described here offer plenty of options in style, color, pattern, and texture, while standing up to the everyday needs of a working kitchen.

Ceramic Tile
Pros: Wide variety of colors and shapes and can be continued on walls. Heat-resistant. Easy to clean.
Cons: Grout lines may stain. May chip or crack (but repairs are easy).
Cost: Low to moderate; designer tiles raise the cost significantly.
Tips: Choose hard, nonporous, glazed vitreous tiles for counters.

Concrete
Pros: Very durable and heat-resistant. Unlimited tints and textures, and can be cast in interesting shapes.
Cons: Requires regular resealing to minimize staining.
Cost: Moderate to high
Tips: Each fabricator brings a unique style to the finished product, so check out the work of several before selecting one.

Granite
Pros: Durable and heat-resistant. Rich colors. Available in glossy or honed (matte) surface.
Cons: Requires regular sealing to minimize staining.
Cost: Moderate to high
Tips: If you don't mind grout lines, granite tiles offer a similar look at less expense.

Laminate
Pros: Wide range of colors, textures, and edge treatments. Easy and quick to install.
Cons: Subject to scratches and denting if abused. Hot pans will leave scorch marks.
Cost: Low to moderate
Tips: Laminate can offer the look of stone, wood, or metal at a more affordable price.

Quartz Surfacing
Pros: Many colors and textures, including the look of natural stone. Stain-, chip-, and heat-resistant, and does not require sealing.
Cons: Cost
Cost: Moderate to high
Tips: An excellent low-maintenance alternative to natural stone.

Solid-Surfacing
Pros: Wide range of colors and textures. Can include a molded-in sink and drainboard to eliminate seams.
Cons: Subject to scratches and heat damage (though easily repaired).
Cost: Moderate to high
Tips: Many customization options, which will drive up the cost. Solid-surfacing veneer offers a similar look at lower cost.

SINKS

Materials

Acrylic, Composite, or Solid-Surfacing. Molded-through color hides scratches. Offers the look of stone without the weight.

Enameled Steel or Cast Iron. Wide range of colors. Enameled steel may chip; cast iron is more durable.

Stainless Steel. Inexpensive and durable (the lower the gauge, the thicker the steel). Brushed and satin finishes are easier to keep looking good.

Stone. Includes slate, soapstone, concrete, fireclay, and granite. Beautiful but costly. Requires sealing.

Styles

Standard. 33×22 inches with two bowls of equal size; large/small configuration also available. Optional extra deep bowls (10 to 14 inches) available.

Single Bowl/Farmhouse. Typically 25×22 inches; smaller than standard sink but best for soaking large pans. Farmhouse models are extra deep and have an exposed front apron; available in vintage and contemporary designs.

Triple Bowl. Wider than standard sink with a variety of size and depth options. Third bowl is usually small and used for food prep and disposal.

Bar or Prep. Small single-bowl units are ideal for installing in an island or near a beverage area.

Corner. L-shape double-bowl sink designed to be installed at the junction of two counters. Spacesaving size is useful in smaller kitchens.

Sink Buying Tips

• Flatter basins and straighter sides accommodate larger loads.
• Check that the holes in the sink's deck match the faucet you want.
• Look for accessories such as rinse baskets, cutting boards, and utensil storage.
• Decorated bowls offer designs similar to ceramic tile.

FAUCETS

Styles

Bridge Faucet. Vintage style where handles and spout are linked by a tube.

Gooseneck Faucet. Tall, arched spout makes it easy to fill a tall pot.

Pullout Faucet. Combines a faucet and sprayer in one unit.

Postmount Faucet. Installs with a single hole in the sink or countertop.

Pot-Filler Faucet. A wallmount, extendable spout; delivers cold water only. Usually located near a cooktop and used for filling large kettles.

Faucet Buying Tips

• Single-handle models provide easiest temperature control.
• Metal braid hose on pullout faucets is durable and offers maximum flexibility.

APPLIANCES

Refrigerators

Size. Minimum of 12 cubic feet for the first two household members and 2 cubic feet per additional person. The more you cook at home or entertain, the larger the unit you should consider. Standard refrigerators are 24 to 36 inches wide and 30 to 36 inches deep. Built-in units, which are cabinet-depth (24 inches), and commercial-style models range up to 48 inches wide.

Configuration. Units with top-mount freezers come in the widest variety of sizes and prices. Bottom-mount freezers keep fresh foods at a more convenient level. Side-by-side styles offer a higher proportion of freezer space but less convenient

Commercial-look glass door refrigerator

access. Both side-by-side units and bottom-mount models with French doors have narrower doors, making them suited to narrow spaces.

Features and Style. Automatic icemakers, in-door water and ice dispensers, and fully adjustable shelves are widely available. Specialized options include multiple temperature and humidity zones, quick-chill or quick-thaw compartments, and slide-out shelves and baskets. Doors clad in wood-finish panels and stainless steel continue to be popular. Newer options include see-through glass doors, retro-look exteriors, eye-popping colors, and easy-care faux-metal finishes with the look of stainless steel and bronze.

Energy Usage. Look for the Energy Star designation, which indicates a model that exceeds federal energy standards by at least 15 percent. The Energy Guide label helps you compare estimated operating costs.

Dishwashers

Capacity and Size. Standard units are 24 inches wide and deep and are designed to be installed under a counter. Larger, smaller, and "portable" models are available for special needs. Capacity ranges from 10 to 16 place settings. Water usage ranges from 4.6 to 9 gallons per normal load; the less water used, the less expensive the operating costs.

Cleaning Features. You'll find multiple wash/dry cycles at all price levels. If you spend more you can get sensors that adjust water temperature and washing cycles based on how dirty the dishes are.

Useful Options. Electronic controls are generally more reliable than mechanical dials. For long life look for a stainless-steel interior. Adjustable (or removable) racks and specialized holders for stemware and cutlery help maximize loads. An Energy Star label indicates a model that uses at least 41 percent less energy than federal standards require.

Ranges, Cooktops, and Ovens

Electric or Gas? Consider both options before making a final decision. Gas appliances cost more initially but are less expensive to operate. Many cooks prefer the precise control and high heat output of gas cooktops, but new technology offers similar abilities in electric models. Baking aficionados tend to prefer electric ovens—and especially convection ovens—for their even heat. Can't decide? Consider a separate cooktop and wall oven or a dual-fuel range that combines a gas cooktop with an electric oven.

Ranges. The standard four-burner range measures 30 inches wide and is either drop-in/slide-in (for installation between cabinets) or free-standing (with finished side panels). Commercial-style ranges can be up to 60 inches wide with six burners or a combination of burners, grill, or griddle. Oven capacity varies, so check each with your largest pan. Double-oven ranges combine a standard-size oven with a separate smaller oven above.

Cooktops. Modular cooktops offer interchangeable cartridges that let you customize with grills or griddles or even combine gas and electric modules. Electric burners have seen the most technological advances. Higher-cost smooth glass cooktops combine precise and quick temperature control with a sleek, easy-to-clean surface. High-end options include 200-Btu "simmer" burners and 16,000-Btu (or higher) burners for searing meats and boiling water.

Wall Ovens. A separate oven makes sense in kitchens with two cooks. Wall ovens range from 23 to 36 inches wide and 1.8 to 5.25 cubic feet. Consider a convection feature for faster, more even baking; another speedy option: ovens that combine microwave and conventional baking.

Options to Consider. For ranges and cooktops:
• Sealed burners for easy cleaning
• Automatic reignition
• Continuous grates that allow you to slide pans safely from burner to burner
• Sensors that adjust active-element size to the diameter of the pan

For ovens:
• Self-cleaning or continuous cleaning
• Temperature probe for precise roasting
• Convection feature that speeds cooking and produces a more even temperature throughout the oven cavity

Specialty Appliances

Warming Drawers. These compact units keep cooked foods at the perfect holding temperature. Ranging from 24 to 36 inches wide, many can accommodate up to four dinner plates. Units with a wide range of temperatures— 82 to 250° F—can handle everything from proofing dough to holding soup.

Refrigerated Drawers. If you do a lot of entertaining or want two fully equipped work centers, a one- or two-drawer unit can provide extra cold storage in a compact space.

Warming drawers

Icemakers. For crystal clear ice look for models that offer "fractional freezing," a system that eliminates impurities.

Wine Refrigerators. Small units fit neatly under cabinets and hold 25 bottles or more at the right angle and temperature. Some larger units also offer separately controlled sections that match the requirements of different wines. Some units sound an alarm if the temperature changes dramatically.

Steam Oven. Cooking with steam produces moister meat, fish, and poultry and more colorful, full-flavored vegetables. Though faster than regular ovens, steam ovens do not brown food.

Dishwasher Drawers. Stack two of these units and they occupy the same space as a traditional dishwasher but allow you to run smaller loads more efficiently. Or use one for small loads or overflow from a large meal.

High-end ranges require large-capacity vent systems.

2

Living and

See more of this addition on page 86.

Family Rooms

No space plays more roles than a living or family room. By day, it's the recreation hub for the kids. After dinner it's the perfect spot to unwind with a good book. And come the weekend it's the place to gather with close friends. This chapter shows how to plan a living room or family room addition that keeps all your options open.

■ Plan for Family Activities

Think about functions, not just space, when you plan. Consider the activities you want to encourage rather than simply the extra space you think you need. This 18×23-foot family room addition was planned with three distinct functions in mind: watching TV, reading, and doing art projects. The designer set aside specific zones around the perimeter of the room for each activity, planning not only the features each activity needed, but the light and space requirements as well. The result: a family room that serves the whole family.

The addition replaced the home's original cramped family room and extends out an extra 13 feet. Subtle design cues help blend old and new. For example, like those in the original house, the windows in the addition vary in size and are generally vertical rectangles.

Arched windows exploit the gable space created by the cathedral ceiling. In addition to providing light and views, the windows combine with built-in seating to produce a pleasant reading nook. The doorway on the left leads to the pool.

As you plan your family room addition, remember that your needs will change over time. Provide for flexible storage that can be reconfigured to accommodate everything from a preschooler's doll collection to a teenager's video games. Provide a compact conversation area for an intimate gathering while including enough space for your biggest holiday celebration. Keep your furniture arrangement options open by considering the number and locations of windows and doors. By planning an addition with multitasking in mind, you'll minimize the need to spend money revamping the space later on. And you'll maximize the pleasure you get spending time with your family.

Perfect for lounging with a beverage and a good book, the window seat includes drawers designed to hold game equipment and supplies for family art projects.

FLOOR PLANS ▨ addition area ▨ new structure

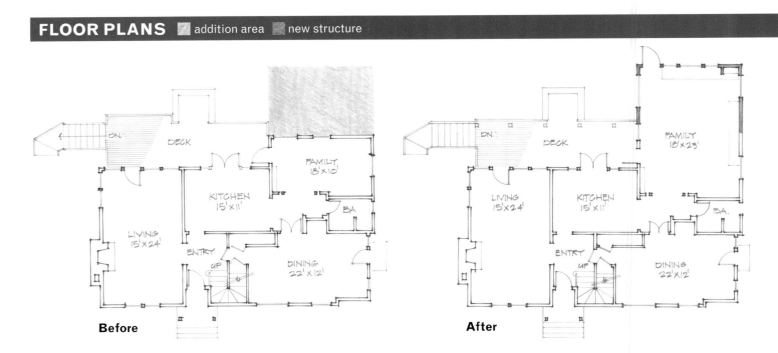

Before

After

The old family room provided little space for family activities. The size of the new room—along with lots of built-in storage—accommodates a variety of activities and allows for plenty of flexibility in furniture arrangement. The addition was in the same spot, which minimized the need to change the existing structure to accommodate the construction. Like the original room, the addition has a doorway leading to the deck; an additional door provides direct access to the patio and pool.

HOW TO FRAME A ROOF

The construction of a roof can be among the simplest parts of framing an addition or it can be the most complex. Builders typically adopt one of two basic approaches:

Site-built (also called stick-built) roofs are put together piece by piece from lumber cut at the job site. This traditional approach allows the maximum flexibility in creating the shape and look of the roof. Site-built roofs are also best if you want to have attic space. The shed and hip roofs illustrated here (**2** and **3**) are examples of typical site-built roofs. The downside to this approach is that it takes longer and costs more.

To save time and money, many builders use prebuilt structures called roof trusses to form the framework of the roof. Trusses combine ceiling joists (the horizontal members that form the ceiling) and rafters (which support the roofing) into a single unit that can be loaded on a truck and shipped to the job site for quick installation. A variation, the scissors truss **(1)**, features sloped rather than horizontal ceiling joists to allow for a vaulted or cathedral ceiling. Because they are built indoors with precision-cut lumber, trusses are uniform in size and shape.

1. Truss roofs are easy to install but may not be suitable in situations requiring complex roof shapes.

2. Shed roofs are easy to build but are not always the most aesthetically pleasing.

3. Hip roofs are a popular traditional shape, particularly in European-influenced designs.

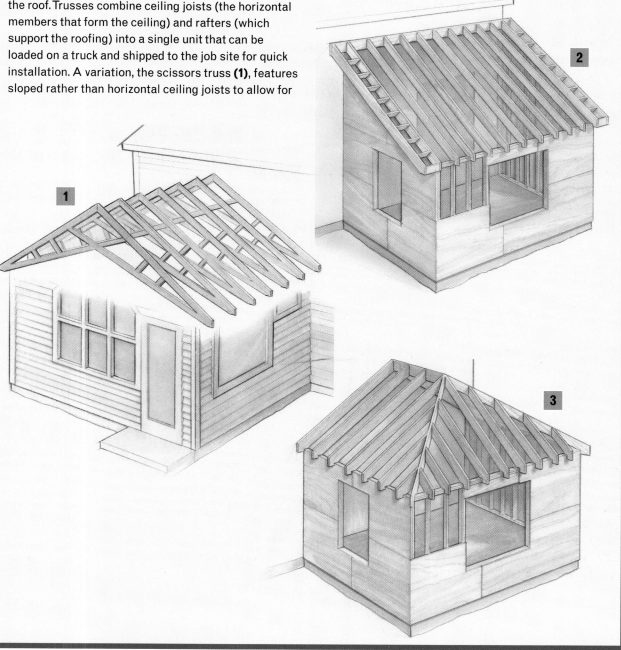

■ Working within Zoning Restrictions

Look for creative options. Sometimes the solution to a problem is obvious. In the case of this too-snug former fishing shack, the problem was a zoning regulation that forbade extending the home's foundation closer to the river running behind the house. The solution: Use the existing patio as the foundation for a new family room. Along with revamped first and second floors, this new space turned an eyesore into a cozy haven with a river view.

The low-slope roof of the family room addition is in keeping with this home's origin as a simple fishing shack. The right third of the addition was built on an existing concrete patio. Sliding doors provide seamless access to the backyard and dock.

Named for the view it encompasses, the river room brings natural light and a feeling of spaciousness to the rear portion of the house. Draperies hung near the ceiling make the room seem a bit bigger by creating the impression of taller windows.

Removing a portion of a wall opened the kitchen to a revamped rear foyer and the river room. The tile-topped island serves as both a workspace and a casual dining spot.

FLOOR PLANS ▨ addition area ▨ new structure

Recasting the existing laundry as a foyer integrated the room addition into the home's floor plan. Moving the laundry meant reducing the size of the kitchen, though the new island makes up for the loss of counterspace and provides an eating area.

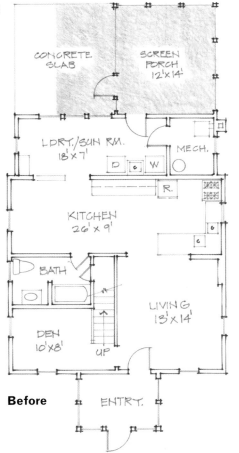

CONCRETE SLAB

SCREEN PORCH 12'x14'

LDRY./SUN RM. 18'x7'   D W   MECH.

R.

KITCHEN 26'x9'

BATH

DEN 10'x8'   UP

LIVING 13'x14'

Before   ENTRY.

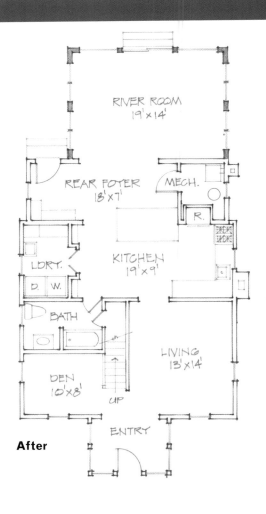

RIVER ROOM 19'x14'

REAR FOYER 18'x7'   MECH.

R.

LDRY.   D W.

KITCHEN 19'x9'

BATH

DEN 10'x8'   UP

LIVING 13'x14'

After   ENTRY

Zoning restrictions need not derail your addition plans. You may be able to obtain a variance, which requires pleading your case before town officials and, in some instances, your neighbors. In some situations you can extend new space beyond an existing foundation without violating the rules. Even if you believe your situation is hopeless, an architect or designer may be able to show you ways to add less but smarter space, gaining the functionality you need without running afoul of your neighbors—or the law.

HOW TO FRAME A WALL

Whether you are planning for one window or a dozen in an addition, the elements of an exterior wall are the same. Here's a quick look at those pieces:

Wall framing. Working flat on the plywood subfloor, carpenters form the basic wall structure by nailing studs **(1)**, usually 2×4s or 2×6s, to a soleplate **(2)** and a top plate **(3)**. (After lifting the wall framing sections into place, a second top plate will be used to join the sections and add extra strength.)

Window openings. Carpenters frame precisely sized openings in the wall structure for windows. Extra studs **(4)** are added to the sides of each opening to make up for the loss of support from the missing studs. Additional support comes from a thick header **(5)** of lumber and plywood above the opening.

Exterior finish. Plywood sheathing **(6)** is nailed to the exterior side of the wall to add rigidity. At this point the roof or a second story is framed and sheathed. Later, weatherization of the structure is completed by attaching siding **(7)**, roofing, and other exterior cladding materials. In some cases your builder may sandwich insulation or a weatherizing "house wrap" between the sheathing and siding.

Utilities and insulation. After windows are installed and the structure is weathertight, wiring and outlet boxes are installed in the stud cavities, which are then filled with insulation **(8)**.

Interior finish. The final step is to install gypsum wallboard **(9)**. Trimwork comes after the walls are finished and painted.

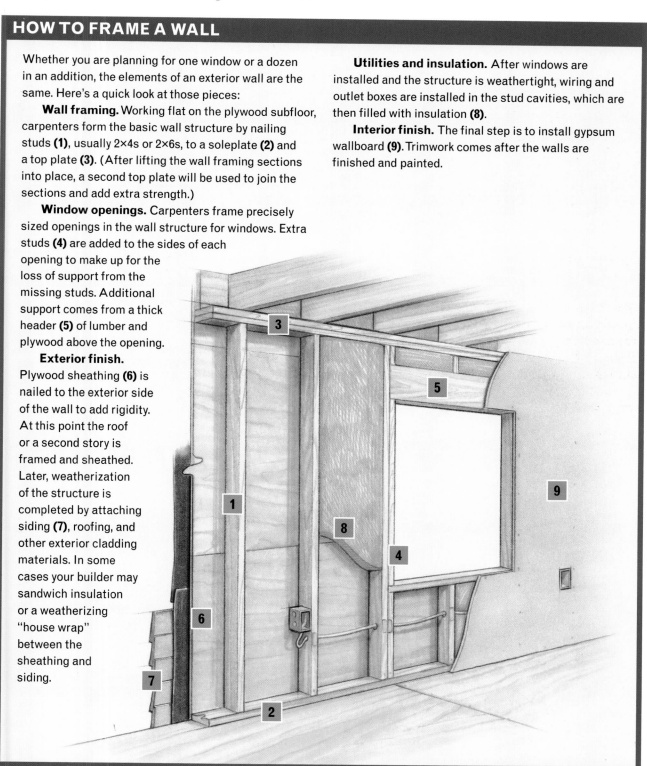

■ Reconfigure for Function

Know when to go with a pro. A professional designer's greatest strength is an ability to seamlessly blend all the elements of a remodeling project. Adding a family room to this 1940s-era Cape Cod house could have been a matter of simply tacking extra space onto the back. Instead a talented architect transformed the interiors into a flowing space that includes a new family room, a breakfast area, and a remodeled kitchen. The blending occurred not only on the inside— the new addition creates a more beautiful exterior too.

Floor-to-ceiling windows help make the breakfast room a favorite place for family gatherings. The wood beam above the granite-topped island marks the spot where the addition connects to the existing house.

A jog in the wall provides a visual break between the family room and breakfast area within the housewide addition. The spaces created by the addition help eliminate the home's chopped-up floor plan and play an integral role in revisions throughout the main level.

A minor jog in the addition's wall sets the stage for a pair of gables echoing the traditional Cape Cod roof design. The twin peaks add plenty of visual interest to the facade without overwhelming it in a sea of siding. The simple hip-roofed portico is also a practical period touch.

The custom-built media center divides the addition from the living room. Transom windows above the flanking doorways help channel light from the addition's windows into the front portion of the house.

The convoluted outline of the addition and the revisions to the floor plan offer a hint of the complexity of the remodeling process. (Contractors remodeled the second floor as well, and the home's mechanical and electrical systems were updated.) To minimize disruptions the family moved to a rental property during the nine-month renovation, which added 1,550 square feet to the 5,300-square-foot home.

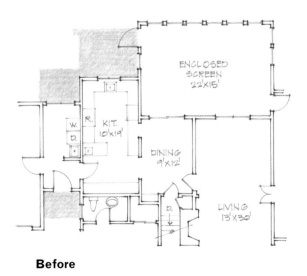

Before

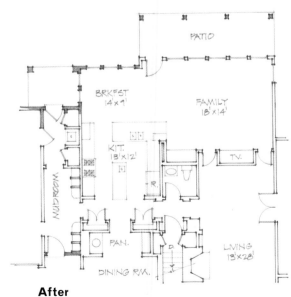

After

Smaller changes suggested by the architect also helped enhance the home. The original mudroom entrance, squeezed between the garage and kitchen, was barely large enough to contain a washer/dryer pair and a couple of coats. Closing in more of the space in front and adding just 5 feet to the back resulted in a truly useful dirt-catching entry to the house. Ideas like these convinced the homeowners to ignore the advice they had been given: Tear down the house and start from scratch. As a result, they have a house with the character they craved without giving up the features they wanted.

Spacesaving storage options, such as open shelves and built-in benches, allow this mudroom to fulfill its mission despite being less than 6 feet across. The flooring is wear-resistant weatherproof slate.

■ Make Room for Entertaining

Materials matter. Planning a successful remodeling involves more than sketching out four walls and filling them with paper furniture cutouts. You also need to think carefully about the materials that will best suit the space you are creating. This garden room addition sports a slate floor, the perfect match for a room that blends four-season comfort with a patio ambience. Though roughly the same cost as hardwood, slate tile offers benefits such as a cool touch during warm summers and lasting beauty that's as easy to clean as vinyl—a fact that commends the material for use in high-traffic areas.

French doors open wide to blur the line between the new garden room and the stone-paved patio. The airy arbor shades the stone patio and produces an ever-changing shadow pattern that's pleasing year-round.

Ceiling beams create visual texture overhead; slate tile creates tactile texture underfoot. Placing the fireplace on the endwall of the 25-foot-long room creates a focal point for the conversation area that doesn't compete with the outdoor view.

A major impetus for adding space was the lack of a dining room in the existing house. This end of the garden room hosts a stunning country French tableau that's perfect for activities ranging from board games to formal dinners.

Arches frame a view in the hallway leading to the addition. Removing a section of built-in storage units from the existing kitchen allowed the development of this direct path.

FLOOR PLANS ▨ addition area ▦ new structure

The old floor plan needed only minor changes to accommodate the addition. The rearranged kitchen kept the original sink window, which had overlooked a three-season porch that was removed during construction. Removing a storage unit created a direct path to the addition, eliminating the zigzag flow through the living room. Keeping the addition's shape simple helped control costs, allowing for upgraded trimwork and a new stone patio.

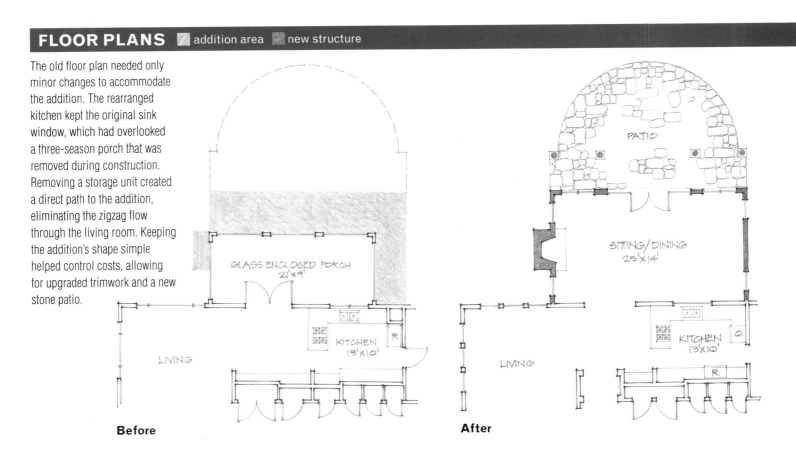

GLASS ENCLOSED PORCH
21'X9'

KITCHEN
13'X10'

LIVING

Before

PATIO

SITTING/DINING
25'X14'

KITCHEN
13'X10'

LIVING

After

The safest route to picking materials for a remodeling job is to take your cue from what you have now. An alternative is to change the existing space to match what you want in the addition. In this house, for example, the slate used in the new sitting/dining room was also used in the rearranged kitchen and hall. Bringing the color and texture of the stone into the original part of the house helps integrate the addition more fully and gives a facelift to the existing structure as well.

HOW TO INSTALL STONE TILE FLOORING

Slate flooring is a premium material that will last as long as the house and, with proper care, will develop a patina that grows more beautiful over the years. Installing a stone floor isn't significantly different from installing ceramic tile. In both cases, a very rigid supporting structure is critical to avoid flexing that will lead to cracking. Because stone flooring is more irregular than molded ceramic tile, your supplier may recommend a wider spacing between the stones than is typical for ceramic tile.

Most contractors who install stone flooring will select one of two basic approaches. A traditional mortar bed installation (bottom) is favored by many contractors who say it produces a more durable floor. This technique starts with a layer of tar paper (1) to protect the subfloor (2) from moisture. A thick (about

¾-inch) layer of mortar (3), reinforced with wire mesh, provides a rigid underlayment for the stone, which is adhered to the mortar with thinset adhesive (4). The last step is to grout the spaces between the stones (5).

A simpler system (below), and one better suited to the do-it-yourselfer, replaces the mortar bed with cementitious backerboard (1), which is installed on the subfloor with screws and adhesive (2). Joints between the sheets of backerboard are bridged with mesh tape (3) to provide a smooth surface. The stone is attached to the backerboard with thinset adhesive (4), then grouted to fill the joints (5).

Stone flooring doesn't have to be sealed, but sealing is generally recommended to minimize stains and protect the surface.

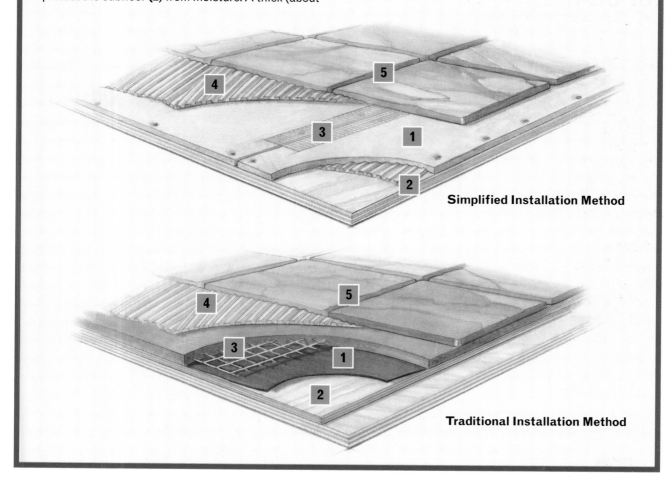

Simplified Installation Method

Traditional Installation Method

■ Working with a Sloping Site

Change (of level) can be good. A downward sloping site is a challenge for anyone planning an addition. Increasing the height of the foundation invariably leads to an ungainly expanse of wall or, worse, a sea of lattice over a supporting framework. To avoid these eyesores, go with the flow and build the addition at grade level and plan a pleasant transition from old to new. This new family room is set three steps below the adjoining kitchen, making the add-on at the front of the house seem like an organic part of the structure rather than something tacked on later.

Appearances are particularly critical for the front of a house. Building the addition at the same level as the kitchen would have given the room a much larger profile, drawing attention away from the rest of the house.

Descending the three steps leading from the kitchen to the family room addition makes for a grand entrance. For a look at the kitchen side of this remodeling project, see pages 40–41.

The reserved face of the built-in storage units steals none of the attention from the fireplace, which is faced in warm-tone slate. The blue and white decor echoes the clean country palette of the adjacent kitchen.

FLOOR PLAN ▦ new structure

Incorporating a dining island into the kitchen and eliminating the separate dining area left plenty of space for the transition area between the kitchen and steps to the family room. The relatively large difference in level made it critical to allow plenty of landing space at the top and bottom of the stairway.

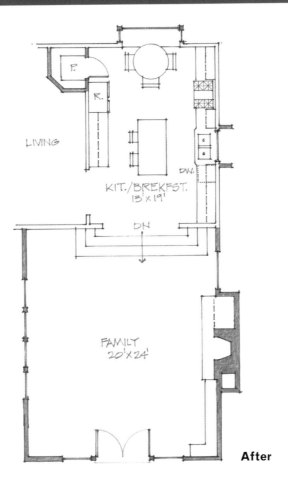

LIVING

P.

R.

DW.

KIT./BREKFST.
13' x 19'

DN

FAMILY
20' x 24'

After

A sloping site influences much more than the appearance of an addition. You must also consider the optimal configuration for the foundation, the flow of water along and around the slope, the need for engineered retaining walls, and the type of landscaping best suited to preventing erosion. For these reasons it is critically important to consult an architect or engineer when planning an addition on a site with a major change in grade level.

HOW TO SELECT A PREFAB FIREPLACE

A fireplace is a surefire winner in any family room. Today's manufactured fireplaces are relatively inexpensive, and their light weight and cool-touch exterior surfaces make installation easy. These prefab fireplaces are also energy-efficient; some can even heat a portion of your home.

If you haven't shopped for a fireplace lately, you'll be amazed at the changes in the past few years. Electric models with simulated, but still realistic, "flames" are perfect for locations where you don't want the hassle of installing a vent or chimney.

But if only a real flame will do, modern gas-fired units offer the ultimate in convenience. You'll find three basic types of gas fireplaces:

1. Direct-Vent. These fireplaces have a clear, virtually invisible glass panel over the front of the firebox. A coaxial (pipe within a pipe) vent behind or just above the firebox supplies outside air for combustion through the outer pipe and exhausts waste products through the inner pipe. These fireplaces may also circulate room air around the outside of the firebox to provide heat to the room.

2. B-Vent. These units have an open firebox like a traditional masonry fireplace and offer larger openings than direct-vent units. B-vent fireplaces draw combustion air from the room and have a vertical pipe (flue) that exhausts waste gases above roof level. Some units circulate room air around the firebox for heating.

3. Ventless. If you want to avoid putting a hole in your wall or roof, you can purchase units that do not require outside venting. Although generally safe, ventless units add substantial amounts of water vapor to the room air, which can lead to mold and mildew problems if used frequently in humid climates.

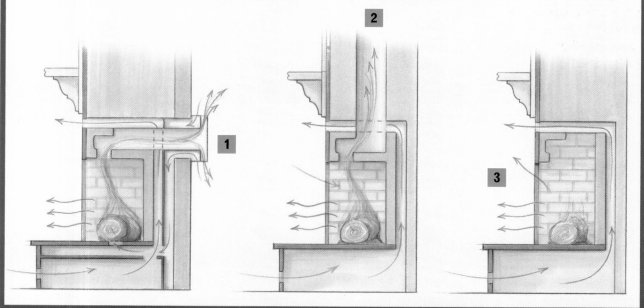

The planning process is identical whether you're adding a wide open family room or an intimate formal living room. Factor in the ages of your family members and the uses you plan for the space. It also makes sense to consider your family's personality—your tolerance for noise and clutter, for example.

Here are the critical issues to consider when formulating ideas:

Activities. The more you ask of a space, the larger it needs to be. A room destined to host intimate conversation or quiet reading could comfortably fit into a 10×10-foot space. Conversely, a family room that has to accommodate art activities, preschool play groups, teenage video gaming, and holiday gatherings might feel cramped in anything smaller than

18×24 feet. Personal preference ultimately determines the optimal size for living and family rooms, but start with the functions you want to accommodate rather than a particular room size.

To experience this "inside out" approach to planning, start by determining what furniture, storage, lighting, and floor space you'll need for each activity. For example, one "activity module" might be centered on a game table. Another module might be designed for relaxing with a book or newspaper. Using paper cutouts or a computer design program, arrange each of these activity modules around the perimeter of your planned room to see how well they fit.

Allow some space between modules so they don't feel hemmed

in. Use design tricks such as columns, half-walls, and area rugs to define specific functional areas without reducing the room to a group of closed boxes.

Noise Levels. Rooms that generate lots of noise should be isolated from rooms that need quiet. For example, sounds from a family room should not be seeping into nearby bedrooms. Likewise, you might not want kitchen commotion intruding on your enjoyment of music in the living room.

To control sound locate a noisy addition well away from quiet zones or ensconce it behind a set of French doors. Or use special construction systems that minimize the transmission of sound through walls, floors, and ceilings. These systems range from the inexpensive—adding

The need to accommodate a special item, like this grand piano, is one reason to consider an addition.

insulation to shared walls—to more sophisticated approaches that combine special wall components and even specific decorating materials.

Storage. Let the functions of the room determine the amount and type of storage you need but plan on a mix of specialized storage (for DVDs, for instance), which is more space-efficient, and general storage, which offers flexibility. Include open and closed storage in the mix so you can display attractive items and hide clutter.

Built-in storage uses space more efficiently than freestanding units, but it also limits furniture arrangements. Confine built-ins to one wall unless you are certain that you'll never part with that 84-inch sofa. Another option is to incorporate storage into built-in furniture, such as shelves under a window seat.

Amenities. Amenities that add comfort and function bring an addition to life. A few to consider:
• Specialty lighting. This might mean something as simple as a mood-changing dimmer or accent lights to highlight prized artwork. Task lighting is critical for reading and playing games.
• Bar or beverage center. A prep sink, coffeemaker, and small refrigerator can turn a tiny living room into a soothing retreat for harried grown-ups.
• Media center. This can be as simple as a decent radio on a shelf or as sophisticated as a top-of-the-line built-in high-definition home theater. (See the chart above for sizing guidelines on home theater screens.)

HOW BIG A SCREEN?

If a high-definition TV is part of the plan for your family or living room, use this chart to determine how large a screen you should consider. For sophisticated installations, consult a home theater specialist.

Viewing Distance	Optimal Screen Size (measured diagonally)
5 to 8 feet	30 inches
6 to 10 feet	40 inches
8 to 12 feet	50 inches
10 to 15 feet	60 inches
12 to 18 feet	70 inches

• Computer station. If a PC is in your plan, ensure that you have the right wiring and outlets within easy reach.
• Fireplace. Perhaps the most traditional amenity of all, a fireplace adds a focal point that warms the heart and, if it has a heat-circulating feature, warms the room as well.

Windows are a key consideration for a living or family room. When planning their placement, consider the impact on furniture arrangements and the use of video and computer screens.

3

Bedrooms

Imagine an island of calm in a frantic world or a private place to reconnect with someone special after a busy day. This chapter reveals the secrets to creating a personal space you can enjoy as much during your waking hours as during your trips to dreamland.

See more of this addition on page 106.

and Bathrooms

■ Rethink the Floor Plan

Dare to trade spaces. Additions often expand a section of the house but keep the function the same. Cramped kitchens become larger kitchens while remaining more or less in the same place. Here's a remodeling project that takes the opposite tack. Just about every part of the house is flip-flopped. One of the most interesting changes is the jump made by the master bedroom. Originally shoehorned between the garage and living room, the room made a leap to the very back of the house, a move enabled by a modest addition.

Equally available to the living room and two bedrooms, the small courtyard provides a tranquil retreat for family and visitors. Tough sailcloth shades protect interiors from the rays of the harsh midday sun.

The old master bedroom offered a "view" of a narrow side yard. The new bedroom, relocated to the back of the house, offers ready access to a lovely shaded patio, perfect for enjoying the balmy southern California weather. Matching wood valances conceal hardware for privacy shades and vertical blinds.

Thinking outside the box is a great exercise for anyone considering a remodel. Experiment with completely new arrangements—on paper or on your computer. And when the plan *almost* works, consider whether a small addition might make all the difference. That's what happened here. Combining two existing bedrooms didn't create enough space for a master suite, but when one wall was pushed out 7 feet, everything fell into place. Worried the plan won't work? A designer or architect can tell you if your ideas are on the right track. A good builder can help you decide whether you can afford it.

Clean-lined maple cabinetry, a granite counter, and steel sinks add up to a decidedly contemporary look in the master suite. It, in turn, matches the built-ins and fixtures found throughout the house.

FLOOR PLANS 🔲 addition area ■ new structure

Before remodeling, this ranch home suffered a host of floor plan sins. The tiny entry opened directly into the living room; the kitchen and garage weren't on speaking terms; and the master suite seemed like an afterthought. The new plan flips the garage to the left side, moves the kitchen into the garage's old position, and places the master bedroom in an enlarged space at the rear of the house. Even with the addition, living space in the house is a modest 1,800 square feet.

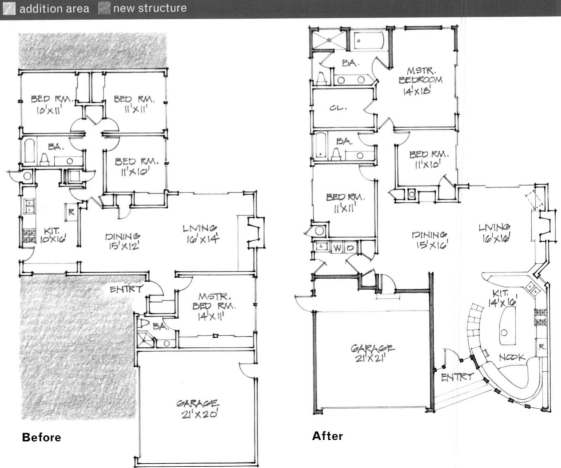

BED RM. 10'X11'
BED RM. 11'X11'
BA.
BED RM. 11'X10'
KIT. 10'X16'
DINING 15'X12'
LIVING 16'X14'
ENTRY
MSTR. BED RM. 14'X11'
BA.
GARAGE 21'X20'

Before

BA.
MSTR. BEDROOM 14'X18'
CL.
BA.
BED RM. 11'X10'
BED RM. 11'X11'
W D
DINING 15'X16'
LIVING 16'X16'
KIT. 14'X16'
GARAGE 21'X21'
ENTRY
NOOK

After

A skylight bathes the master bath in daylight. The half-wall divider between the tub and shower, required for the showerhead plumbing, offers a bit of privacy. The door at the back leads to the toilet compartment.

Tucking into Tiny Spaces

There's always a way. If you think a home has no room for expansion, imagine one that's barely the width of a sidewalk away from its neighbors. This 900-square-foot San Francisco cottage may be hemmed in, but it was still possible to add a bedroom. The solution: Expand a partial attic with a dormer, then provide access with a skinny circular staircase. Sure, the lack of a bathroom upstairs is a drawback, but what a view through the twin French doors that lead out onto a small rooftop terrace!

The narrow path leading to the house is flanked by neighboring homes. A sliver of the new dormer is visible behind the scroll ornaments. The home's main entry is reached by taking a left turn at the plant table.

A new bedroom appears in the attic thanks to an 18-foot-wide shed-roof dormer. The dormer's face, on the left, is pierced by two pairs of French doors, which gather light and views and provide access to a small terrace that sits above the lower level. The black pole is the upper end of a spiral staircase.

White walls and ceilings and a limed vertical-grain Douglas fir floor diffuse light throughout the room. Custom cabinetry provides adequate storage without eating up a lot of floor space.

FLOOR PLANS ■ new structure

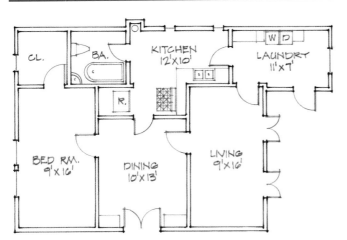

Main level before

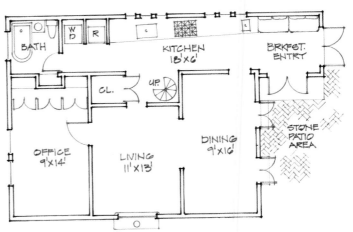

Main level after

Although the house was gutted and rebuilt, the overall outline of the main floor remained virtually unchanged. That's not surprising given the proximity of neighboring homes. Installing a traditional staircase was impractical, so a narrow spiral unit was added for access to the new upper-level bedroom. A slim gas fireplace in the living room provides a heat source suited to the San Francisco climate.

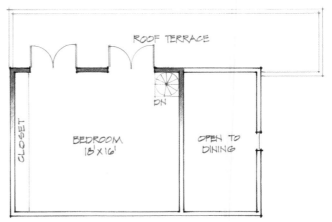

Upper level after

Adding the dormer was probably the simplest part of this remodel, which involved securing the house with a belt so it could be raised enough to build a new foundation. New floor joists, beefed-up structural members, and a layer of insulation were also a part of the plan—not to mention a reorganization of the main-level floor plan. You might say this home is a poster child for the "No House Left Behind" movement. It is certainly proof that creativity and gumption can make just about any remodeling dream come true.

HOW TO INSTALL A SKYLIGHT

One of the quickest ways to add energy and personality to an attic space is to install a large skylight. In addition to bringing in much-needed light, a skylight also can provide a view and ventilation at a much lower cost than a dormer or other addition.

Each skylight manufacturer provides detailed installation instructions for its products, but many are a variation on this basic approach, which assumes a skylight sized to fit neatly between existing rafters.

Working from the underside of the roof, mark the center of the skylight location by driving a nail through the roof. From the outside, use the driven nail as a reference point to outline the rough opening. Remove shingles from the area, then re-mark the rough opening and cut it out. Install a header (**1**) at the top and bottom of the opening and attach the skylight frame (**2**) to the roof. Secure roofing felt and flashing (**3**) around the frame to prevent leaks. Attach the sash (**4**) to the frame and caulk joints as needed, then attach shingles around the skylight. Finish the inside of the installation with drywall (**5**) on the exposed faces of headers and rafters.

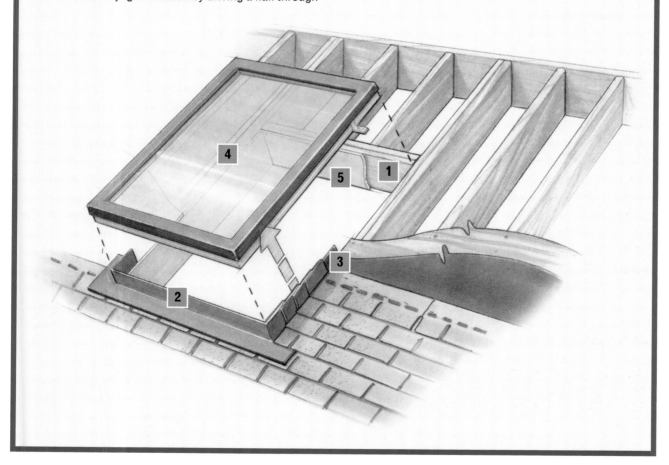

■ Bump Out to Create a Master Suite

Get more space by going over the edge. Additions don't have to be confined to the foundations. Bumping out an addition a few feet beyond the foundation is a time-honored technique for finding a few extra square feet for a room, and it can work just as well upstairs as on the main level.

This second-story bedroom acquires master suite proportions with the addition of a 2-foot-deep strip that extends from the supporting wall of the room below. Expanding the space still farther is a window seat nestled into its own 2-foot-deep extension—a bumpout on a bumpout!

The new addition follows the symmetry of the first-floor design. In addition to creating more space for the master suite, the addition's overhang provides a measure of weather protection for the windows and French doors below.

The new master suite extends a second-story addition that was added across the front half of the house in the 1970s. The majority of the addition was bumped out 2 feet beyond the supporting wall below; the section housing the window seat was bumped out another 2 feet.

The compact home office next to the bedroom can be closed off with pocket doors to provide privacy or to block out noise.

FLOOR PLANS ▪ new structure

Bumping out the addition meant that the builder would not have to make expensive structural changes to the previous addition. Not having to move the staircase eliminated what would have been a disruptive change affecting both upper and lower levels. Changes were made to the old addition to accommodate the new master bath.

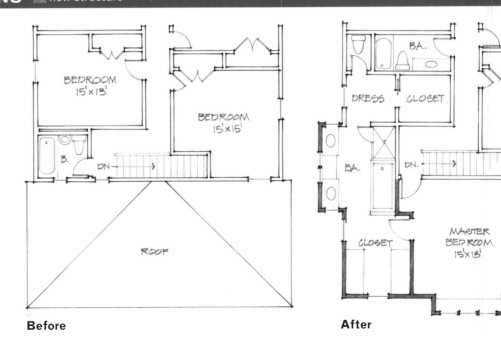

Before

After

A second bumpout adds elbow room in the narrow master bath. The twin sinks and vanities are set in the 2-foot-deep recess. The custom cabinetry, tongue-and-groove wainscoting, and wide moldings reflect the Arts and Crafts style of the 1920s-era home.

Bumpouts save money by reducing the size of the foundation needed or, in the case of a second-story bumpout, by eliminating the need to make costly changes to a home's lower level. But they may offer another advantage: In many communities the setback—the minimum distance between the house and the lot line—is based on the location of the foundation. In these cases bumping out beyond the foundation allows a slightly larger addition. Of course all good things have their limits. Bumpouts deeper than 4 feet require extensive and expensive supports, eliminating most or all of the cost savings.

The Carrara marble used to edge the tub was also used on the vanity tops and in the shower. This vintage-appropriate material blends beautifully with the blue and white palette.

■ Add an Attic Master Suite

The details make it special. The difference between a good remodeling project and a great one lies in the details. While few will realize the thought you put into picking the perfect location for your new master bath, they will immediately appreciate the look and feel of that designer faucet on the vanity. This whimsical master suite, which occupies the upper level of a two-story addition, is a case study in the benefits that flow from paying attention to the little things.

White-painted woodwork and flooring create a restful backdrop for the home's country decor. The staircase just beyond the door leads to a dining room on the first level of the addition.

Custom barn doors painted periwinkle blue add a heaping portion of country flavor to the master bedroom addition in this vacation cottage. The doors are also practical: Their wall-hugging operation preserves floor space without the construction hassle required for the alternative of pocket doors.

Pedestal sinks and black and white floor tile will look good for years to come and are easy to clean.

The claw-foot tub offers a vintage look but is 18 inches longer than the antique version. Other modern amenities include an old-style faucet with a handheld showerhead and a glass shower stall that doubles as a steam room. Windows set in dormers brighten the bath and bedroom.

FLOOR PLANS ▦ new structure

The master suite devotes plenty of room to the bath, a real luxury in a small house. A thoughtful detail in the bathroom is a pass-through that allows direct deposit of dirty clothes in the laundry room hamper.

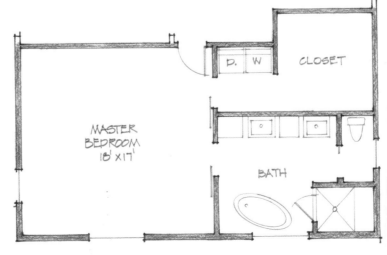

D. W   CLOSET

MASTER BEDROOM 18' X 17'

BATH

After

When it comes to remodeling, the details that count fall into two categories. First there are the elements that please the senses. In this case that includes the heft of solid-wood doors, the subtle texture of beaded-board paneling, and the bold statement of wide moldings. Then there are the practical details, such as dual medicine cabinets in a shared bathroom and a conveniently located laundry hookup. While planning your own remodeling, follow the lead of the masters. Work through the big issues early, and remember to pay attention to the details that will come last.

HOW TO PLAN A DORMER

Dormers are among the least expensive ways to add useful square footage to living spaces tucked under a steeply sloped roof.

1. Shed dormers are best for adding a significant amount of floor space because they can be as wide as the house itself and still have a pleasing appearance. You can maximize the space created by a shed dormer by designing it to fit the entire space between the ridge board and the exterior wall of the house.

2. Gabled dormers have a peaked roof, which lends them a special charm and personality that are particularly appropriate for traditional-style homes. Though they can be large, gabled dormers are most often used to create nooks or niches or to funnel light into an attic space. Outfitted with windows, small gabled dormers can even be installed in cathedral ceilings to provide extra daylight to the room below.

The illustrations show the typical framing for shed and gabled dormers. Careful planning and top-notch carpentry skills are required to create the basic framework. Attention to detail is also critical during finish work to ensure that the joints between the dormer and roof are completely weathertight. For these reasons, it makes sense to hire professionals with extensive experience in building dormers in your area.

■ Add an Upper Level

Bedrooms aren't just for sleeping anymore. OK, they never were just for sleeping, but too often the amenities that turn a bedroom into a retreat are little more than an afterthought. When planning a master bedroom addition, try a three-step approach. Step 1: Provide enough space for a comfortable chair or two. Step 2: Incorporate entertainment options into the plan. Step 3: Include a connection to the outdoors. A textbook example of this approach is this second-story master suite, which helped revitalize a modest two-bedroom ranch home.

The cedar-sided bumpout provides visual relief from the expanses of stucco in the Asian-inspired facade, which was redesigned as part of a whole-house remodel. Like the original structure, the second-story addition has a flat roof suited to this dry California location.

The bed snuggles into a niche that faces the street. Numerous windows provide light, air, and views but are high enough to maintain privacy. Built-ins keep reading material close by and provide a reclined headboard for comfortable lounging. Nearby a pair of chairs creates an intimate conversation group.

To make the most of a bedroom, plan as if it were a family room. Identify the activities that will occur there—reading, watching movies, exercising, whatever—and include the amenities those activities require. Flexible storage is critical, but so are a solid lighting plan and provisions for wires, speakers, and other electronic equipment. If you like relaxing with morning coffee, include a compact coffee bar and a pleasant (and private) outdoor space to enjoy it.

FLOOR PLANS ▨ addition area ▧ new structure

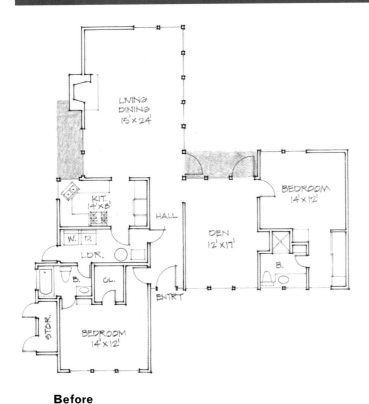

Before

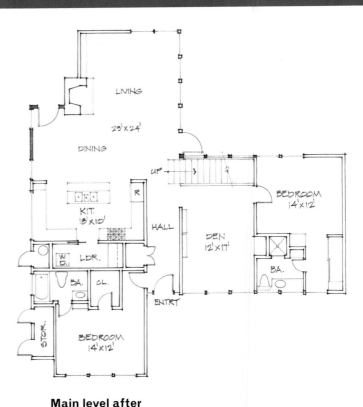

Main level after

The bedroom addition was part of an extensive remodeling project. On the main level a small addition allowed the cramped, closed-in kitchen to expand and open to the living/dining space. A second main-level addition houses the new stairway that provides access to the second-story addition. The home's original ceiling structure was not designed to support a second story, so new joists and support beams were installed.

Upper level after

The tiny rooftop deck offers just enough room for a bistro set and makes the ideal setting for morning coffee or a romantic dinner for two.

The custom media center opposite the bed includes
closed storage and display space plus built-in speakers
and a floor-level subwoofer for theater-quality sound.
The cabinets also provide a measure of privacy from the
windows in the stairwell behind.

Amenities for baths go far beyond the familiar jetted tub: oversize soaker tubs, full-body showers, steam generators, heated towel bars, foot-soaking tubs, aromatherapy infusers, heated toilet seats, and light-therapy units are just a few of the indulgences you can include. The options for turning a master suite into a luxurious retreat are limited by little more than your imagination and budget. The key to success is to start planning early and decide on your priorities. Builders will tell you it's much more expensive to add a feature after construction starts than to plan for it from the beginning.

A skylight in the master bath's shower infuses the enclosure with soft light.

Maple plywood cabinets provide a contemporary setting for twin sinks. Leaving space under the cabinets keeps this narrow space from feeling like an alley.

■ Move a Wall to Make a Bath

Minor changes can lead to a major upgrade. When planning an addition, why not look at changes that could enhance the original space as well? That's the story behind this stunning master bath remodel. The original bathroom included a skinny (5×13-foot) vanity area, a compartmented toilet, and a shower stall—but no tub. Adding a jetted tub increases the room's versatility and improves its function. To make space, one wall was pushed out about 5 feet, enough to hold the tub and, as a bonus, add more walk-in closet space.

Though retiled, the shower stall was unchanged by the remodeling. The new vanity offers a comfortable place to sit and apply makeup.

With a color palette inspired by the Italian coast, this revamped master bath gained some breathing room because the wall opposite the twin sinks was pushed out 2 feet. A small makeup vanity and a storage cabinet take up the newly liberated space.

Adding those extra square feet did nothing to cure the vanity area of its claustrophobic width. To overcome that problem, a short existing wall was moved 2 feet into the space behind it. The result: a bathroom that suddenly feels twice the size. If you're thinking about moving (or removing) a wall, remember that moving a *bearing* wall (one that helps hold up the ceiling or upper floor) is a much bigger job than moving a nonbearing wall. Differentiating between the two types of walls takes a little detective work, but a builder or designer can figure it out fairly easily.

The terrazzo tile floor continues the coastal color scheme and provides a long-lasting, easy-to-clean surface. The cabinet next to the makeup vanity is wall-mounted to help the room feel larger.

FLOOR PLANS   ▨ addition area   ▨ new structure

Though once considered cutting-edge, the existing bathroom had begun to show its age. The remodeling plan brought the room into the 21st century with only modest changes. By keeping the existing fixtures in place, the remodeling plan required new plumbing only for the jetted tub. Moving a wet wall—which encloses water supply lines, drains, and vent pipes—is a major undertaking, one that can substantially increase the cost of a remodeling.

DRESSING
9'X11'

BATH
5'X13'

Before

DRESSING
6'X8'

BATH
8'X17'

CLOSET
9'X6'

After

One wall of the toilet compartment was pushed out just enough to hold a jetted tub. The glass tile used here and in the shower stall is a darker shade than the tile used on the counters and was chosen to suggest the color of deeper water.

Planning Guide for Bedrooms

CHOOSING A BATH LAYOUT

Bathrooms come in all shapes and sizes. The layouts shown here illustrate a variety of arrangements designed to save space. Even if you have little room for your bath, be sure to follow the minimum clearances shown in the chart on page 121.

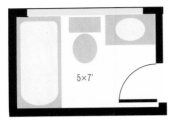

One-Wall Layout
The least expensive full bath concentrates the plumbing in one wall (shown in yellow) and has interior measurements of 5×7 feet.

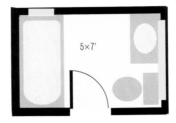

Two-Wall Layout
Although also 5×7 feet, this arrangement offers more room in front of the sink. The trade-off is extra plumbing.

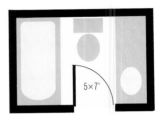

Three-Wall Layout
With three walls plumbed, this 5×7-foot design offers the most counterspace and storage of the three minimum-size arrangements.

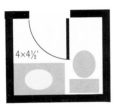

Half Bath
At 4×4½ feet, this design can be tucked into a former closet. An alternative layout puts sink and toilet at opposite ends of a 32×84-inch space.

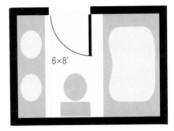

Mini Spa
Though it measures only 6×8 feet, this layout has room for a long counter and a top-of-the-line tub.

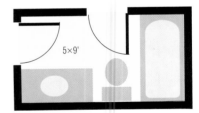

Hollywood Bath
A Hollywood bathroom provides access from two rooms. This design, which measures 5×9 feet, serves a bedroom and a hallway.

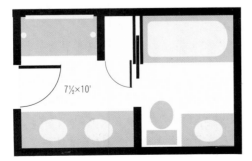

Family Bath
This 7½×10-foot layout is designed to accommodate the needs of an entire family.

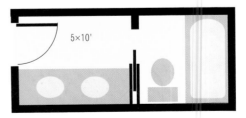

Bath for Two
Putting the tub and toilet in a separate compartment ensures privacy and keeps the shower from steaming up the vanity mirror. This layout measures 5×10 feet.

NUMBERS TO KNOW

Before finalizing your bath addition plans, check to see that they measure up to the recommendations of top bath designers.

	Recommended Minimums	Tips
Aisles and Doorways	32 inches of clear opening for doorways; 36-inch-wide aisles	For wheelchair access allow a 5-foot-diameter turning circle.
Single Sink	15 inches from centerline of sink to any sidewall; 18 inches on each side is preferred	Allow at least 8 inches between the edge of a sink and the end of a counter.
Twin Sinks	Allow 30 inches between sink centerlines	Allow at least 8 inches between the edge of a sink and the end of a counter.
Toilet	16 inches of unobstructed space on each side of the toilet's centerline	Open floor space in front of the toilet should extend at least 16 inches in on either side of centerline.
Toilet Compartment	At least 48×48-inch floor space in front of toilet	Use a pocket door or an outward swinging hinged door. Allow 32 inches for doorway width.
Shower	36 inches wide by 66 inches long	For comfort a shower should be at least 36 inches square.
Counters	At least 34 inches square; standard counter height is 30 to 32 inches	Vanity heights of up to 42 inches are acceptable for tall users.

FIVE WAYS TO MAKE A SMALL BATH FEEL BIG

Provide enough light to dismal corners. Bright, indirect lighting aimed at the ceiling creates a sense of height.

Replace a bulky vanity with a sleek pedestal sink.

Include one or two horizontal lines—such as a row of contrasting tiles or a paint stripe—to lead the eye around the room.

Avoid a mix of materials and keep patterns light and small in scale. This strategy makes surfaces seem larger.

Install a large mirror on one wall to create the sense of a room that's twice the size.

Planning Guide for Bedrooms

BATHROOM SURFACING MATERIALS

The heat and humidity of a bathroom put a lot of stress on materials used for walls, floors, and countertops. Here's a rundown of the best choices to consider:

Limestone counters and floor tiles provide calming color and natural texture.

Flooring
Vinyl. Long-lasting, low-maintenance, and inexpensive compared to other materials
Laminate. Durable and low-maintenance. Proper sealing is critical to prevent water from getting under the floor.
Tile. A lifetime material, but can be very expensive. Use only tile designed for flooring. In cold climates consider underfloor radiant heat.

Wallcoverings
Paint. Inexpensive but requires regular repainting. Use paint with a mildew-resistant additive.
Wallpaper. Inexpensive. May need replacement in five to seven years. Choose moisture-resistant coverings.
Ceramic tile. A lifetime investment with relatively low maintenance. Price varies from moderate to high.
Solid-surfacing. Lifetime investment with low maintenance. Expensive in large quantities and requires professional installation. Best for tub and shower surrounds.

Countertops
Ceramic tile. Moderate to high cost and long-lasting. Grout needs frequent cleaning and resealing.
Laminate. Low cost and easy to maintain.
Stone. Granite and marble are most common. Lifetime investment, but expensive. Requires regular resealing to protect surface.
Solid-surfacing. Long-lasting and low-maintenance. Moderately expensive. Can be purchased with an integrated sink.

MASTER BATH AMENITIES

An upscale bath addition typically returns about 85 percent of its cost, according to surveys by *Remodeling* magazine—not a bad payoff if you enjoy several years of spalike pleasure from your remodeling. Here are some of the most intriguing amenities to consider when planning a bathroom addition.
• Gallery-worthy fixtures such as vessel sinks that resemble art glass bowls
• "Deep heating" far-infrared saunas
• Steam shower compartments
• Extra-deep soaking tubs
• Programmable shower systems with multiple nozzles
• Touch-free automatic vanity faucets
• Toilet with heated seat and built-in bidet feature
• Furniture-quality cabinetry
• Radiant floor heating
• "Bubbling" tubs with a gentler massaging action than standard jetted tubs

Extra-deep soaking tubs let you relax away stresses.

BEDROOM PLANNING GUIDELINES

Bedrooms can be simple or elaborate. Regardless of your goals for your bedroom addition, there are time-honored rules that should guide planning.

Location, location. Privacy and quiet are the hallmarks of a bedroom, and the location you choose should reflect those ends. Bedroom doors should not be visible from public areas such as the entry or living room; nor should the path from bedroom to bathroom subject the traveler to public scrutiny. Keep bedrooms quiet by placing them away from noisy areas (the laundry room, kitchen, or family room) and by using sound-deadening wall construction. Noise travels from bedroom to bedroom too, so pay attention to layout within the cluster of bedrooms. Contain noise by setting closets on shared walls. Or install a bathroom between the rooms but remember that morning showers may intrude on late sleepers in the adjacent bedroom.

Location affects bedrooms in other ways, of course. If children are young, you might prefer a master bedroom near their rooms, or at least on the same floor. Once your kids become teens, no amount of separation might be enough, so weigh your options carefully. Location affects light levels too. East-facing windows will brighten the room early in the day, perhaps earlier than you'd like. A north-facing bedroom will have low light levels year-round; a south-facing room will be bathed in sunshine all

Smart window placement can increase the options for placing a bed.

day. Finally, consider external factors such as the view and external noise levels; you may enjoy the view of a busy street during the day, but rue the noise level at night.

Size. Various federal guidelines and local codes spell out the minimum size of bedrooms—generally ranging from 70 to 100 square feet. Even if your project isn't covered under these guidelines, don't ignore their intent. One way to approach size is to start with the furniture you intend to use (or might someday want) and plan around it. For easy access, allow aisles of at least 3 feet on each side of the bed and 4 feet in front of it. To gain even more usable space from a bedroom, consider adding vertical space to

accommodate loft beds or a small library and reading nook. If TV watching is in your plans, consider how the viewing distance impacts the size of the screen you'll need. (See page 91 for recommendations.) Finally, don't forget to include ample closet space.

Light and ventilation. Building codes set minimum requirements for bedroom windows but may neglect the issue of ventilation. Having windows on at least two walls improves airflow at times when you want fresh air. Work with a designer to develop a lighting plan that includes both general illumination and task lighting for reading, sewing, office work, and so on.

See more of
this addition
on page 130.

Sunrooms

Early in the day these indoor-outdoor zones beckon you to wake up to sunshine and fresh coffee. At close of day they offer a quiet gathering spot for family and friends. In this chapter you'll find some outstanding examples of sunrooms and porches to help you plan your own addition.

■ Bring in Light and Air

Good things come in threes. A well-designed sunroom performs three functions that make a house more comfortable. It funnels natural light deep into the house and gathers cool breezes and fresh air. It also provides flexible space for relaxing, dining, or just enjoying a view. Windows—and plenty of them—are the key to fulfilling these roles. Though it measures only 7×13 feet, this modest sunroom performs all the functions of a much larger space because it has operable windows on all three exterior walls.

The 12×12-foot kitchen was remodeled at the same time the sunroom was added. Installed on the wall farthest from the sunroom, the commercial range is topped by a powerful ventilation hood tucked below a plate shelf similar to the one that rings the sunroom.

A love seat and a small table are enough to outfit this sunroom addition. Tucked between the kitchen and an open porch, the sunroom serves as an extension of both spaces. The double-hung windows that line the addition's three exterior walls are a stylistically appropriate choice for this 1913 cottage.

Homeowners planning a sunroom addition have a variety of window options. For older homes and those in temperate climates, double-hung windows like the ones used in this project provide plenty of light and excellent fresh airflow while maintaining a vintage look. In cold climates, side-hinged casement windows and top-hinged awning windows provide the tightest, most energy-efficient weather seal. Skylights provide daylight and, if they can be opened, a way to vent the warm air that collects at ceiling level. Fixed windows provide a budget-friendly alternative but, because they don't provide ventilation, are not an ideal choice for a sunroom.

Like the sunroom addition the new porch is small, just 8×12 feet. Although protected by a roof, it is otherwise open, allowing plenty of light to reach the sunroom.

FLOOR PLANS ▨ addition area ▧ new structure

A small porch was demolished to make way for the new sunroom and covered porch. Although the footprint of the kitchen didn't change, the space was gutted and outfitted with new cabinets, counters, and appliances. In an unusual move, the refrigerator was taken out of the kitchen and installed in a new pantry/laundry room carved out of a bedroom.

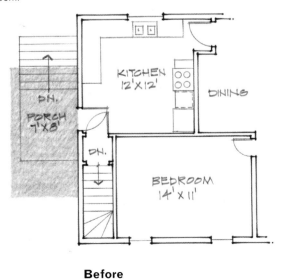

Before

After

Floor-to-ceiling windows might seem a good choice for a sunroom, but they limit furniture arrangements, especially in small spaces. In this room providing wall space under the windows allows a sofa to be placed against the wall.

129

■ Build for Comfort

Allow for sun—and shade. Although windows define a sunroom, they can also be its downfall. Left unchecked, sunlight can quickly turn a pleasant relaxation zone into an unbearable sauna. By incorporating a few elements into the design of a sunroom, this heat buildup can be controlled and even put to good use.

Start with windows designed to block the warming rays of the sun. This type of window typically includes two or three panes separated by air spaces, which slow the transmission of heat through the window. A more effective system uses a combination of low-E glass, which is coated with a thin layer of metal oxide, and argon gas trapped between the panes. These high-tech windows help control heat gain in summer and heat loss in winter yet don't impede light or the view.

With its patio-style terra-cotta tile floor, vintage wicker furniture, and large expanse of windows, this 16×20-foot sunroom addition offers the sensation of being outdoors without the exposure to the elements.

Manually operated awning windows provide an escape route for sun-warmed air while offering some protection against sudden summer showers. Deep roof overhangs shade the glass during the hottest part of the day.

Canvas shades on wires can be drawn to control glare from the roof windows. Because of the amount of glass in the roof, this sunroom required the expertise of a contractor experienced in designing and building such structures.

Wintertime heat gain in the sunroom helps warm the house via an accordion-fold window and a French door. In summer closing the window and door keeps the heated air out of the house.

After choosing the right windows, next consider shading. For vertical windows, roof overhangs provide welcome shade in summer (when the sun is high in the sky) but allow the warming rays of the sun to enter the space in winter. Roof-mounted windows and skylights require their own shading systems. Shades incorporated into the skylight or window are most effective at blocking heat buildup; shades installed below roof-mounted windows diffuse the harsh rays of the summer sun.

Ventilation is the last element in controlling heat buildup. Windows that open, particularly near (or on) the ceiling, allow heated air to escape. Besides encouraging fresh airflow, this natural system of heat control is far less expensive to operate than air-conditioning.

HOW TO BUILD A SLAB-ON-GRADE FOUNDATION

For a modestly sized addition in a mild climate, a slab-on-grade foundation is an economical choice. Unlike a crawlspace or basement foundation, this type of foundation requires minimal excavation. It also eliminates the need for a separate subfloor. Together these factors minimize cost and construction time.

Construction starts with a two-level excavation that is shallower in the center and deeper around the edges of the slab's location. Next comes a supporting layer **(1)** of gravel for drainage, sand, and a moisture barrier.

Next reinforcing materials such as rebar and wire mesh are laid down to strengthen the concrete, which is poured into the excavation, creating a single unit that combines the slab **(2)** and the footings **(3)**. To prevent water from undermining the foundation, a drain system **(4)** is installed around the perimeter of the foundation. Insulation **(5)** around the permeter of the foundation prevents energy loss from the room.

Slab foundations are less practical in areas with deep frost because separate foundation walls and footings must be poured to provide support for the slab, eliminating the cost savings. A hybrid technique called a frost-protected slab uses the extra insulation around the foundation to keep the surrounding soil from freezing.

■ Choose the Right Materials

Durability counts for a lot in sunrooms. The average sunroom is subjected to more wear and tear than most rooms—including extremes of temperature and exposure to dirt and grit tracked in from outside. Finish materials should be chosen with an eye toward toughness and easy cleanup. In this sunroom add-on, the ceramic tile floor was a natural choice. It stands up to dirt and doesn't suffer if a window is accidentally left open during a rainstorm. The walls and ceiling are clad in vinyl beaded-board paneling, which offers a wipe-clean surface that won't require regular repainting. Even the windows are easy (or at least easier) to keep clean thanks to removable grids.

This entry, on the side opposite the grilling deck, provides easy access to the garden from the sunroom. To help the addition blend with the existing house, the clapboard siding and windows were carefully aligned. Landscaping and lattice minimize the visibility of the open space under the addition.

Three walls of windows, a glassed-in gable, and a ceiling that rises to 16 feet at its peak help this modestly sized sunroom addition feel much larger. Double-hung windows provide ample ventilation. Solar-reflective film on the glass helps minimize heat buildup.

The addition's exterior was styled to match the existing house with easy-care vinyl siding and windows. Lush landscaping hides the exposed foundation and makes the addition look as though it were part of the original structure.

Planning a sunroom involves details that extend beyond the surface materials. Even if you use your sunroom only part of the year, it makes sense to include many of the features you would have in other rooms in the house. These include insulation in walls, floors, and ceilings; electrical and cable TV outlets; and energy-efficient windows and doors. If your plans don't include heat or air-conditioning, consider "stubbing in" the ductwork or electrical service you'd need to add these items later. Although these steps may raise the initial cost of your sunroom, they will greatly reduce the cost of upgrading to fully conditioned space in the future.

One of the benefits of an enclosed sunroom is flexibility in furnishings. The leather chair and ottoman, set back from the windows, create the perfect spot for relaxing with a good book and the wonderful view. A good leather conditioner, applied regularly, will protect the upholstery from sun damage.

■ Design for Character

Don't compromise on personality. The majority of sunroom additions are built from prefabricated kits—and for good reasons. The kits are engineered to be sturdy and weatherproof and can be less expensive and faster to install than a fully custom addition. Prefabricated, greenhouse-style sunrooms, however, may not be the best choice if your house is built in a historically inspired architectural style: The greenhouse look will detract from the character of your home. This Tudor-style sunroom addition illustrates the many benefits that come from custom design. Although maintaining the home's character and value is one benefit, there are other pluses as well. Custom designs are better suited to take advantage of particular views or to provide privacy where needed. They also offer the possibility of unique features, such as the rooftop terrace on this addition.

Bold trim and matching brick help the addition blend seamlessly with the original 1920s-era house. Flat-roofed sunrooms were a common feature on homes of this time period, though modern materials greatly reduce the likelihood of leaks. Adding a terrace above extends the home's second-floor living space.

Floor-to-ceiling windows on three sides of the sunroom bathe the addition in daylight. Although the single-pane windows and French doors have a contemporary look, they echo the proportions of the second-story timber-framed windows, and the transoms repeat the shape of the individual panes in the double-hung windows.

Capturing a home's distinctive character in an addition can be a challenge. While a good architect or designer can develop connections between old and new, homeowners should also be prepared to offer some ideas. Check out additions to similar houses in your neighborhood. For a house with an identifiable style—Tudor, Craftsman, bungalow, Victorian—look to books from your home's era for inspirational pictures. Local historical associations often maintain libraries you can browse. Salvage yards in your area may have architectural details and trimwork that would help create an appropriate look for the add-on. But before getting caught up in trying to match everything precisely, remember that the goal is a livable addition. In the long run, a slavish copy may be less satisfying than a design incorporating modern touches that you love.

The arched doorway between the kitchen and sunroom masks a structural beam added to support the opening in the wall. The beaded-board ceiling and wide trim boards around the windows carry the home's character into this new space.

FLOOR PLANS — addition area — new structure

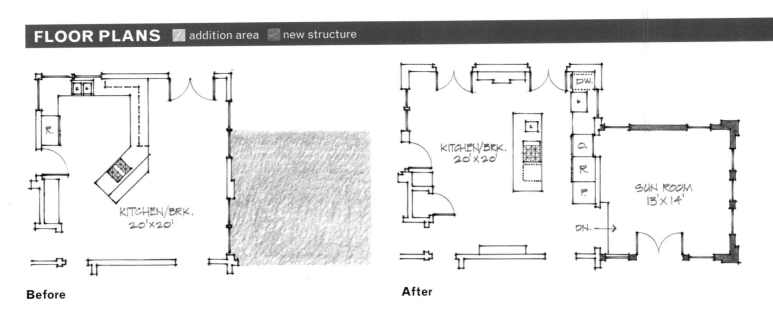

Before

After

The sunroom addition was configured to provide a clear traffic path along one edge of the remodeled kitchen. Although the footprint of the kitchen stayed the same, the space was gutted and outfitted with new French doors leading to the garden.

The sunroom addition offered an opportunity to completely remodel the kitchen as well. The sink, oven, and refrigerator all moved to the outside wall that is now shared with the new sunroom, so the sink overlooks the same backyard view as the addition.

■ Connect to Nature with a Screen Porch

Consider a screen gem. A sunroom is not the only way to help a house connect with its surroundings. This stylish screen porch provides three seasons of comfort—with the help of the stone fireplace—while providing a much more intimate relationship with nature than a glassed-in room would offer. And with its excellent design, this screen porch doesn't look like an afterthought. The traditional construction technique, which is called timber-frame construction, uses beefy pillars and beams instead of modern 2×4s. The result is a rugged yet elegant lodge-style look that is in complete harmony with the architectural style of the 1912 home.

Because the site sloped away from the house, the new porch addition was built on a full-height foundation. The design created space under the porch for a new garage.

A custom-built stone fireplace extends the use of this screen porch. Prefabricated outdoor-rated fireboxes allow the installation of a fireplace virtually anywhere without costly special foundations or masonry skills.

Easing the transition from porch to garden is a dining terrace halfway between the two levels. Although the porch lacks the trim used on the home's exterior, the matching colors allow old and new to blend harmoniously.

French doors provide wide open connection between house and porch. The flagstone floor relates to the natural surroundings and stands up to weather and muddy boots.

All else being equal, a screen porch will cost less to build than a sunroom, but, because the porch is open to the elements, weatherproof materials and furnishings are mandatory. Building a screen porch on an existing deck is a good option, though you need a builder or engineer to evaluate whether the existing foundation is strong enough to support the new construction. Installing a new foundation offers more flexibility, especially if you decide to enclose the porch later on. Whatever approach you take, a critical element of a screen porch is good drainage for water that will collect on the floor. Your builder or designer can devise a system that works with the type of foundation and flooring you choose.

HOW TO BUILD A BASEMENT FOUNDATION

In cold climates, the foundation of a house or addition needs to extend below the frost line. Otherwise, the cycle of soil freezing and thawing will cause the foundation to rise and fall. The depth of the frost line varies, but is generally no more than 4 to 5 feet, even in the coldest climates. In many cases, the extra cost of extending the foundation walls to basement depth makes that a reasonable option. Most builders and architects recommend that the foundation of an addition match the depth of the house foundation to avoid differences in settling between the two structures.

Construction starts with excavation of a hole slightly deeper and larger than the area of the basement. To connect the old and new foundations, the contractor inserts lengths of rebar into the existing foundation. The exposed ends of the rebar are later wired tightly to rebar embedded in the new footings and foundation walls.

The footings (1) are poured first, usually in shallow forms built on the soil surface. If the walls are going to be poured concrete, the builder will construct forms, set up the reinforcing rebar, then call in the concrete trucks to pour the walls (2). For a block foundation, masons will lay the walls on the footings.

A drain system (3) around the perimeter of the footings keeps water from invading the basement or undermining the foundation. Finally, the wall is coated with a moisture-resistant compound, and the surrounding area is backfilled with soil (4). If the exterior of the foundation will be insulated, the insulation will be attached to the walls before backfilling.

The basement floor (not shown) is a concrete slab poured on layers of gravel and sand. Plastic sheeting under the slab protects the concrete from soil moisture.

Once the foundation is sufficiently set, construction of the addition's floor (5) and walls can begin.

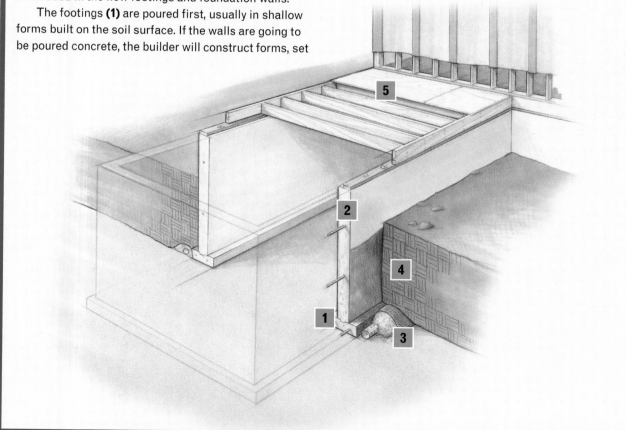

■ Create an Outdoor Room

A simple roof can define a room. When the kitchen in this house underwent remodeling, it offered the opportunity to create an additional room that would take in the nearby ocean view. The solution lay, literally, underfoot. An existing brick patio could be transformed into an open-air room by adding a roof and a few amenities to provide some comfort. The result is this indoor-outdoor room that creates a feeling of shelter but still admits the breeze. Overhead a ceiling that rises to a height of 16 feet at its peak provides protection from rain and sun.

Details such as this wrought-iron chandelier help create the sense that this is a "real" room. The tinted glass shades cast a mellow light after the sun sets.

A partial, or knee wall, of weathered brick anchors one end of the roof, which joins the house at the opposite end. Although completely open on one side, the space gains a sense of enclosure from the house walls and the knee wall.

If the idea of an outdoor room like this intrigues you, consider these suggestions. Install a solid roof to provide protection from sun and rain and to enhance the feeling of enclosure. Include a focal point, such as a fireplace or outdoor kitchen. Attach at least part of the structure to the house to keep access simple and to save on utility connections. Install a floor that won't be slippery when wet; if you want to include a dining table, however, avoid highly textured floors that make it hard to adjust a chair. Remember lighting, electrical outlets, and speakers if you want to enjoy music, and choose furnishings and fabrics that are weatherproof.

Heavy ceiling beams supported on thick posts help create a sense of enclosure and security. Painting everything white makes the framing hardware seem to disappear.

Cushions upholstered in all-weather fabric turn the wide brick knee wall into a comfortable bench. When not being used, the cushions are stored under cover to keep them looking their best.

French doors open from the house to reveal this stunning view. The fireplace, comfortable furnishings, and colorful accessories signal that this is a genuine living space, despite the absence of true walls at the far end and along one side.

Planning Guide for Porches

With their emphasis on natural light, unobstructed views, and connection to the outdoors, sunrooms and porches are among the most popular types of additions. These flexible spaces can serve as dining rooms, family rooms, or indoor garden spaces. And with proper design a sunspace can also help heat a home.

Here are the critical issues to consider when planning a sunroom or porch:

Budget. Because it is unheated, a porch is less expensive to build than a similarly sized sunroom. A big part of the savings may come from using lower quality windows (or using only screens) and little or no insulation. While this can markedly reduce the cost of the project, it also makes it much more expensive to transform the porch into year-round living space later. Even if you don't plan to upgrade, consider asking your architect to design the structure to ease the transition to a year-round room.

Materials. Because they are essentially weatherproof, sunrooms can accommodate any type of flooring or wallcovering used elsewhere in your home. However, if you plan to grow plants, consider the benefits of flooring that won't be harmed by standing water. A porch, particularly a screen porch, must be built with materials that can stand up to water and that won't be harmed by extreme temperature swings from summer to winter.

Location. In most cases the view is going to determine the best orientation for a sunroom or porch. Access to the garden, patio, or deck may also be critical. At the same time, the space should have a logical relationship to the rest of the floor plan. For example, if you plan to use the room for dining, put it near the kitchen; for entertaining purposes, locate it off the living or family room.

Another consideration for location is the climate. In the cold North a south-facing sunroom or porch will be more comfortable in the spring and fall than a room that faces north. In the South the opposite holds true. In any location be sure to have the means to shade large glass areas from the hot summer sun.

Building method. Although porches and sunrooms can be built using traditional methods and

Even though a sunroom is weatherproof, consider furniture designed for outdoor use and select fabrics that are fade-resistant.

materials, sunrooms are often constructed using kits consisting of preassembled sections or specialized pieces that are assembled at your home on a custom-built foundation. The kit approach has many benefits. Construction can go more quickly than a traditional stick-built addition, and there is less chance of leaking—a major consideration in a structure with so many windows. High-quality kits also come with lengthy warranties. The downside of kits is that you are limited to the sizes and styles offered by the builder. While the range of models may be impressive, a kit is unlikely to blend with your home as seamlessly as a custom-designed addition.

Free Heat from the Sun

Passive solar design allows a sunroom to serve as a source of home heating, even in cold climates. Although the design will vary depending on the home's location, all passive solar sunrooms share four key elements:

South-facing windows. Energy-efficient windows allow the winter sun to warm the interior of the sunroom while minimizing heat loss to the outside. Most designs use wallmount windows but not roof-mounted units, which are hard to shade in summer and more prone to heat loss.

Shading. To prevent overheating, deep roof overhangs shade the windows from the summer sun. In winter the sun is lower in the sky, and its rays pass under the overhangs.

Thermal mass. Masonry is used in the floor (and sometimes the walls) to absorb heat during the day, then slowly radiate it back into the sunspace at night. Thermal mass reduces temperature swings, making the sunroom cooler during the day and warmer at night.

Insulation. Relatively high levels of insulation are required to prevent heat loss at night through the walls, ceiling, and floor. It is also important to install insulated covers over the windows.

If you plan to warm your house using a sunroom, include a method for distributing the heat—fans and ductwork or windows and doors between the house and the sunroom.

If possible, site a screen porch where it can catch prevailing breezes. This will make it a more comfortable spot during warmer weather.

Entry

See more of
this addition
on page 158.

Upgrades

A good entry welcomes guests to your home, leading them to the front door and sheltering them from the elements. A great entry also adds character that makes a house stand out from the crowd. In this chapter you'll see some outstanding examples of entry additions that fulfill both of these roles and sometimes even more.

■ Turn Boring into Bold

Make a clear statement. A nondescript entry is like a halfhearted handshake. It signals an attempt to be friendly but lacks genuine warmth. The original entry on this 1920s residence sported a barely there portico, a sliver of roof, and a lonely window in the gable. Passersby were more likely to notice the expanse of siding than the front door.

The highlight of the remodeled facade is the new portico. Though not much deeper than the original entry, the prominent gabled roof and robust trim details suit the style of the house and supply the missing character and sense of welcome. An architect who understands historical styles can help you achieve this kind of effective tranformation.

The entry gains prominence from new leaded-glass sidelights and the robust columns and trimwork of the portico. The new entry was part of a total facade redo that included wider window trim and new roof overhangs.

Though barely deeper than the original, the new portico includes larger, bowed brick steps whose shape echoes the gentle curve of the portico's arch.

The original facade offered little in the way of character, with small windows floating in a sea of siding and a roof that created no sense of shelter.

Give a Flat Front a Facelift

Provide some shelter. Visitors to a home may feel somewhat unwelcome if they are forced to stand in the rain or hot sun while waiting at the door. This simple entry addition was the antidote to the home's original unprotected front door. The new portico is part of an overall facelift that creates a much more pleasing facade. Shutters on the upstairs windows and rough-sawn lintels emphasized horizontal lines that fought the steep roofline. Removing the shutters, replacing the lintels with painted panels, and adding the portico restored the house's storybook character.

The old screen porch to the left of the entry is now a sunroom with windows that match the ones to the right of the entry.

The new entry is tall and narrow, a reflection of the general shape of the house. Matching colors help the new and old construction blend into a single visual unit.

■ Combine Porch and Portico

To create a sociable entry, make a connection. In the past houses commonly included spacious front porches, perfect places for watching the world go by and striking up conversations with neighbors. This combination porch and portico addition revives that friendly tradition. A broad gabled roof beckons visitors to the front entry where new oversize French doors let them know they've arrived. The less dramatic but more enclosing roof above the porch is designed to create a sense of comfort and security. Although clearly defined by large columns, the porch section of the addition is unencumbered by railings or enclosing walls, the better to encourage neighbors to connect with one another.

The front door's arched top distinguishes it from a pair of smaller doors that lead onto the porch from inside the house. A ceiling fan above the seating area provides a welcome breeze on hot, muggy days.

In the original facade, the entry was sometimes hard to spot within the march of the windows.

New intersecting gables added to the garage and house visually balance the new porch and portico. They also make for a more interesting overall appearance.

09

■ Relax the Style

Enhance what you have. The original entry on this stately Colonial served its purpose, directing visitors to the front door and sheltering them when they arrived. Adding a front porch across the width of the facade not only added outdoor living space but also changed the style of the home from formal Colonial to friendly farmhouse. The roof of the new porch leaves the upstairs windows unobstructed and is punctuated in the center by a slightly enlarged version of the original portico. The result maintains the perfect symmetry of the original house but with a warmer, more inviting appearance.

Smooth painted trim and flooring give the entry and porch addition a finished look. To shed water efficiently, the floor slopes slightly away from the house.

New landscaping and brick terraces create a wonderful sense of arrival as guests approach the house.

The original facade was attractive but a bit imposing.

The new portico extends over a pair of wing walls flanking the new front steps. The barrel-vaulted ceiling is paneled to match the flat ceiling over the twin porch sections. Decorative columns conceal the structural supports for the new roof. The brick steps match the masonry foundation.

■ Simplify for a Formal Look

Sometimes the porch is the problem. As pleasant as a front porch can be, it tends to rob adjacent rooms of daylight. That was one reason the new owners of this former summer cottage decided to remake the front facade. The ever-so-slightly off-center front door also ruined the home's otherwise classic symmetry. So off came the porch (and the beach-stripe awnings), and on went a centered entry. The updated look is far more elegant than the original, yet still in character for the 100-year-old house. The star of the show is the flat-roofed portico and enlarged entry, which trade the slouchy look of the original for a more formal yet welcoming look.

Pleasant but busy is probably the best description of the house before the facelift.

The new entry gives the modest home a more imposing visage. To complete the transformation, the small addition on the left received a matching roof makeover.

■ Redesign for Craftsman Style

For a radical redesign, enlist help. It's difficult to imagine a more complete transformation than this one, an ordinary split-foyer home turned into an Arts and Crafts-style spectacular. It shows how any home can be recast by carefully chosen changes—and it shows what a talented architect can do for you. The new entry addition was a major component of this redesign. The massive stone pillars and soaring timber framework make for a majestic entry that's in perfect scale with the height of the house.

Switching from painted clapboard to natural cedar siding set the tone for the facelift, but the new entry ensures that the front door doesn't get lost in the woods. Mixing in a variety of new rooflines reinforces the sense of the care and handcraft at work in the house.

It took real vision to see in this generic split level the starting point for the current house.

Details like the crossed timbers of the entry repeat the shapes used in the new rooflines.

Planning Guide for Entries

Every entry to a home has two sides, each with its own set of functions. The exterior of an entry provides a clear and easy connection between the public space outside a home and the private space within. The interior portion provides a comfortable transition from the world to the more intimate spaces of a home. Although these descriptions may sound esoteric and theoretical, in fact they are simple to achieve and pleasant to experience.

Here are the critical issues to consider when planning entries:

Visibility. The location of the main entry should be obvious to arriving guests. The traditional way to accomplish this goal is to add a porch, stoop, or vestibule that makes the entry project from the rest of the house, creating contrast between the entry and the exterior. Modern designers sometimes create contrast by recessing the entry. If you can't physically update an entry, improve it by painting the door a contrasting color, adding decorative elements above or around the door, or using shrubs to call attention to the entry. At night a brightly lit entry is welcoming. Whatever combination you choose, the more dramatic the contrast between the entry and its surroundings, the better.

To ensure that your guests can reach the front door without having to cross the lawn, add a hard-surface walkway—at least 60 inches wide to allow two people to walk abreast comfortably. Here too contrast is a good way to draw visitors. Punctuate the entrance to a walkway with a decorative object or plant and provide enough light in the evening to avoid accidents.

Shelter. Once a visitor arrives at your front door, the inevitable

The primary entry should reflect your home's personality.

Visual cues such as the brightly painted front door and broad walkway help this welcoming entry stand out.

wait ensues until someone comes to let them in. Make that delay more pleasant by providing shelter from the elements. A porch or portico is the traditional way to achieve this, but an awning, trellis, or arbor can work too. The sheltering element should be large enough to protect at least two visitors from rain or hot sun. Ideally you should be able to open a storm door without forcing your guests back out into the elements.

Transition. The inside portion of an entry—whether a foyer or something more modest—must help visitors (and family) transition between indoors and outdoors. The most awkward entries open directly into a living space. If you can't carve out a separate space for an entry, create boundaries by adding a partial wall or divider screen and a section of contrasting flooring just inside the door.

The most important amenity for an entry area is an ample coat closet, ideally not overstuffed with dog food, brooms, and sports equipment. Lacking a closet, use wall pegs or a coat tree. A bench is a wonderful touch, especially during boot season. The flooring should be resistant to water and dirt but covered with a large (at least 3×5-foot) easily cleaned mat to catch the worst of the mess. The entry should be well-lit at all times; a nice touch is a separate light for the closet.

Beyond the functional aspects, the entry should also serve as an introduction to your home's personality. Incorporate decorating elements—paint colors, framed art,

collectibles—that you use elsewhere in the house. A console table with a mirror may fill this role, but avoid letting decorative items crowd the space. Elbow room is the most welcome luxury in an entry.

Secondary Entries

The concepts applied to a primary entry also work for other entries to your home. Although more likely to be used by family than guests, these

access points must be convenient and functional. Ideally secondary entries include their own coat closets, hard flooring, and mats. For the ultimate in convenience, consider adding a mudroom, complete with a bench, storage for outerwear, and a cleanup center with a sink.

A secondary entry should offer plenty of storage for bulky outerwear and boots. Wall pegs allow quick access to coats and give damp rainwear a chance to dry.

See more of
this addition
on page 190.

Additions

A two-story addition doubles the amount of new space you can tuck under one roof. Though these expansive add-ons present a range of challenges, they also provide opportunities to enhance a home on many levels. This chapter illuminates the benefits of taking remodeling ambitions up a notch and presents solutions to the most common challenges.

■ Find Bonus Living Space

Seize your opportunities. Adding a ground-level room to your home—perhaps a family room like the one grafted onto the back of this 1893 Victorian-style home—also creates the opportunity to add upper-level space. Here an open-air retreat that connects to the master bedroom tops off the addition. Building this bonus living space costs much less than adding a fully enclosed upstairs room, and it can be used through much of the year. Another plus is that the two-story gabled facade is more in step with the existing structure than the typical single-story shed-roof addition would have been.

A neat covered porch provides the perfect transition from the new family room to the backyard garden. The second-level deck and spa enclosure take advantage of space that would otherwise be wasted above the new family room.

As in many old homes, the main floor is several feet above grade level. To ease the transition to the back garden, the new 12×13-foot family room is approximately halfway between the existing main level and the grade level; stairs from the back porch complete the transition.

The spa enclosure provides a modicum of privacy while providing protection from the weather. Sealed beaded-board paneling and cedar flooring stand up to the humidity and reduce the amount of maintenance required.

Adding an upper level to a single-story addition offers a variety of benefits over creating the same amount of space on a single level. The most obvious savings lie in foundation and roofing costs, but plumbing, wiring, heating, and electrical costs may also be reduced. Ongoing maintenance and utility costs will also be lower if the two-story approach reduces the square footage of exterior wall exposed to the elements.

Of course not every one-story add-on can (or should) be transformed into a two-story project. But if you expand your plans intelligently, you might find that an upper-level space can be put to good use, either as fully enclosed rooms or as an outdoor living space with bird's-eye views.

FLOOR PLANS ▨ new structure

Getting to the backyard from the kitchen originally required following a circuitous path through the small back porch. The new family room addition provides a more pleasant and direct route. On the upper level, the larger deck connects the master bedroom and spa.

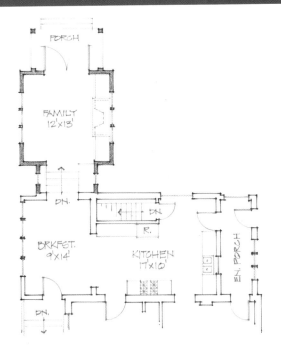

Main level after

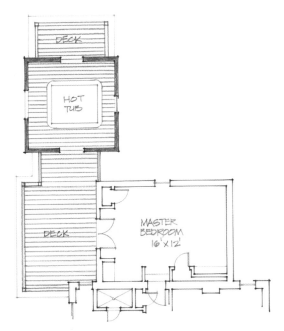

Upper level after

The upper-level retreat includes a large new deck above the breakfast nook. French doors allow the master bedroom, deck, and spa to function as a single flowing space.

■ Build Out and Up

Tailor each space to meet your needs. It's tempting to think of a two-story addition as a box (the addition) glued to the side of another box (the existing house). But unless the goal is two identically sized rooms stacked one on top of the other, this approach has its limits. Another tactic is the one taken at this small vacation home. A small two-story addition combines with a small upper-level addition to individualize the amount of space on each level.

A new porch shelters the home's main entry, which was created during a revamp of the main level. The upper-level addition, which connects to the two-story addition, is behind the porch.

The new living room occupies the lower level of the two-story addition. The portion of the room to the right of the fireplace is part of the original house. The French doors behind the sofa lead to a large new deck.

The goals for this remodeling project played a direct role in the planning process. The aim was to create a comfortable master suite and a fourth bedroom to accommodate frequent summer guests. The main level needed a bit more breathing room but not nearly as much new space as the bedroom level. So the architect developed a plan that included a small two-story addition housing the relocated living room and new bedroom and connected it to an upper-level addition housing the new master bedroom.

Moving the main entry required reorienting the stairs to provide direct access to the upper level.

FLOOR PLANS [ ] addition area [ ] new structure

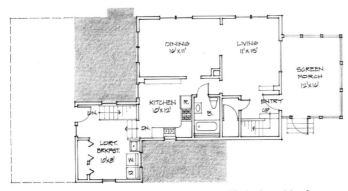

Main level before

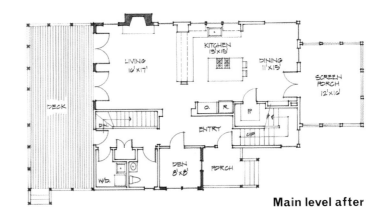

Main level after

The two-story addition was nestled next to the single-story breakfast room. A second addition was built above this room. Another small addition houses a den and entry porch. During the remodeling, the existing house was gutted to the studs, then provided with upgraded mechanicals, new windows, and a revised floor plan.

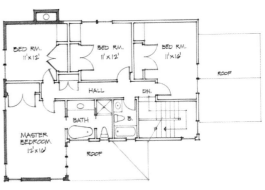

Upper level before

Upper level after

HOW TO PLAN A STAIRCASE

A two-story addition may not always require adding a new staircase, but if your plans include one, you'll need to plan carefully. The design of staircases must meet local building codes to ensure that they are safe and comfortable to use.

Staircases are complex carpentry projects with numerous parts, which may be why many builders opt for prefabricated units they can quickly install at the job site.

Although the look and arrangement of the finished product varies widely, most staircases include the same basic parts. These include stringers **(1)**, which support treads **(2)**. Most stairs also include risers **(3)**, though open-tread stairs are popular for contemporary design. Tread caps **(4)** may be hardwood or carpeted. Finally there are various trim pieces, such as railings or balusters (not shown), that enhance safety and create a finished look. Staircases designed to be carpeted may substitute particleboard for hardwood for the treads and risers.

Tradition and building codes control the dimensions of treads and risers as well as the position of railings. Treads are typically 10 to 11½ inches deep; the deeper the tread, the more comfortable the climb. Risers are generally no more than 7¾ inches tall. For a typical straight staircase in a house with 8-foot ceilings, that means a staircase length of 11 to 14 feet; for 9-foot ceilings, add another 2 feet of length.

If you don't have room for a straight staircase, an L-shape or U-shape staircase might be the answer. Like all staircases, these alternative arrangements are controlled by local codes, so you will face some limitations. Their biggest drawback is the extra difficulty in moving furniture up and down them. For extremely tight spots, specify a spiral staircase. Not all communities permit them because the pie-shape treads are more likely to cause a misstep.

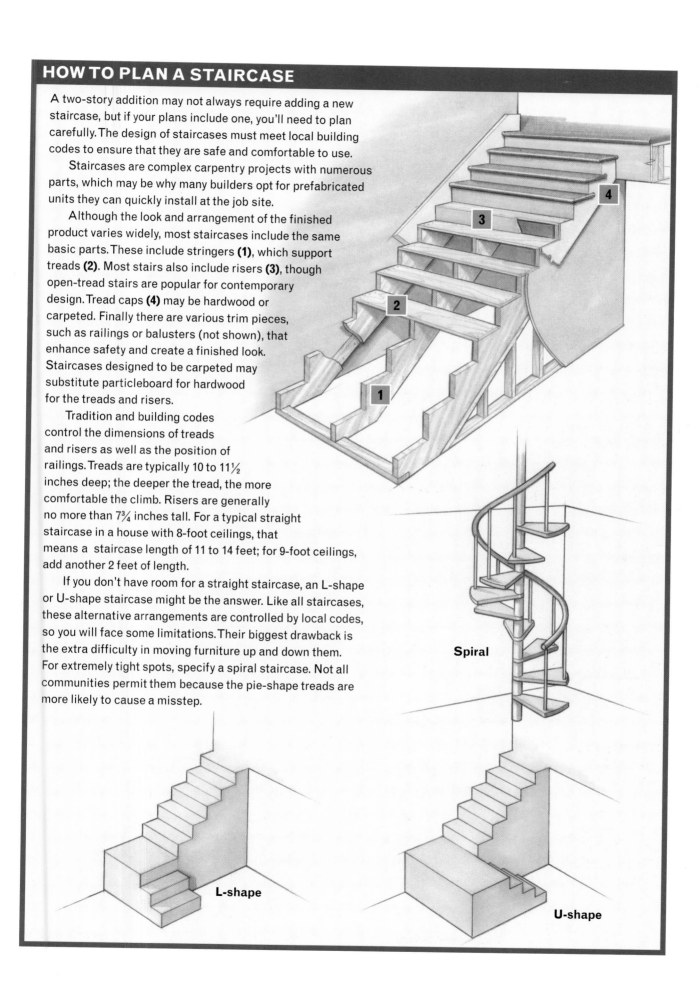

Spiral

L-shape

U-shape

There are almost endless options for tailoring each level of a two-story addition. In this home the new living room borrows space from the existing house to create space that's larger than the new bedroom directly above it. Another way to add less space on the upper level is to frame the addition in the classic story-and-a-half profile, with a room tucked under the gable roof. Adding a dormer or skylight can keep this space from feeling dark or hemmed in. If you need more space upstairs than down, design the lower level with a smaller room and a covered porch or patio.

The open floor plan on the main level blends the dining room, kitchen, and living room into a single flowing space. This view, from the dining room, extends out the French doors to the new deck off the living room.

The farmhouse sink fits perfectly with the home's rustic decor. A flip-open step behind the toe-kick to the left of the sink helps small kids reach the countertop.

The kitchen was moved to the back of the house and made larger and more open. To save money the builder used stock windows to craft the doors of the see-through cabinets.

Save money by configuring new space to meet rather than exceed your needs. A more tailored approach may produce an addition that blends well with your home and your neighborhood. Discuss a wide range of options with a designer or architect and a builder. Cutting a room's size in half doesn't cut the construction cost in half, nor does it automatically produce a more pleasing exterior. In the end an open mind is the best tool you can bring to the remodeling process.

The new guest bedroom, occupying the upper level of the two-story addition, is a soothing retreat. Horizontal wainscoting and a painted pine floor offer a restful backdrop for the country decor.

The master bath sits above the original location of the kitchen. In most cases, stacking "wet" rooms (kitchen, bath, laundry) makes it more economical to install water supply lines and drains.

Originally the home's primary entry, the screen porch offers views of the nearby lake. French doors connect the porch to the relocated dining room.

■ Update a Classic

Proportion matters. The sheer mass of a two-story addition can easily overpower the original house. This 1,360-square-foot addition doubled the home's size, but it is so well designed, it actually enhances the character of the house. Although selecting matching cedar siding and divided-pane windows helps blend old and new, the real key to success is the way the architect broke down the facade of the addition into a set of smaller forms. These varied "boxes," shapes, and rooflines lend the addition a less imposing—and more intimate—appearance.

To help the addition blend into the Shingle-style home, the architect broke up the facade into smaller shapes but tied them together with an arbor that spans the width of the addition. The cupola at the new roof peak recalls an ornamental feature that was common when the house was built in the 1920s.

The new family room occupies one end of the addition's main level. The woodburning
fireplace is the focal point of the room. The French doors lead to a new arbor-shaded patio.

Architects and designers use a variety of strategies to help a large addition seem as though it belongs with the original structure. One option is simply to retain the same basic shape and extend an existing wall and roof to make the house wider or longer. A second approach is to copy the form of any existing extensions or additions. If a radically different design style for the addition is the goal, the architect may separate the new space from the original house, connecting the two structures with a short enclosed passageway. In some cases, the location of the addition is governed by site conditions or setback rules, which may also influence the designer's strategies.

Despite the austere look of the commercial range, painted walls, cherry cabinets, and quartersawn oak floors give the space a jewellike appearance.

FLOOR PLANS ▨ addition area ▨ new structure

The addition required only a handful of changes in the original floor plan. With the kitchen relocated to the addition, the old kitchen was converted to a library. The old dining room was slightly enlarged by moving a basement stairway to the addition. And the original powder room was moved into the addition to create more room in the entry foyer. Upstairs the addition was grafted onto the existing house with little more than a new hallway and a relocated family bathroom.

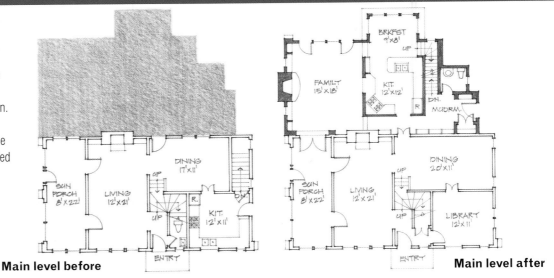

Main level before

Main level after

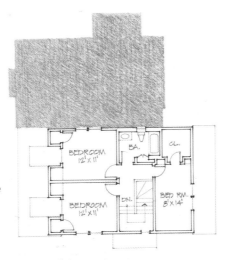

Upper level before

Upper level after

The middle third of the addition's main level is occupied by the kitchen. In a sharp break with current trends, it is only 12 feet square. The stairway to the left is new, linking the kitchen to the addition's upper level.

Building a large, two-story addition is likely to be as expensive as buying another house with the same features and size. And it runs the risk of pricing the house far above the market value of its neighbors. It makes sense to carefully consider moving as an alternative to adding on. If you're committed to the neighborhood, you love your lot, and you love the house, however, then the investment may well be worth it.

A vanity and shower stall share the compact master bath with the tub, a single sink, and the toilet. Although built in, the vanity seems more like a piece of furniture because it's topped by a framed mirror and sconces.

Nestled into a bumpout overlooking the backyard, the whirlpool tub sits under a ceiling that rises 15 feet to the small windows in the rooftop cupola.

On the upper level of the addition, the master bedroom sits above the family room and even has a fireplace in the same spot. The arch motif above the fireplace was inspired by similar arches in the main-level sunporch.

■ Restoring Character

Approach remodeling slowly. "Act in haste and repent in leisure" is an apt warning for anyone planning a major remodel, and it's particularly good advice if you've just bought a house with the intention of remodeling before moving in. Living in the house awhile before embarking on changes allows you to discover firsthand how well the rooms suit their purposes, how traffic flows, and how light moves through the house during the day. Only after experiencing the house on a daily basis can you discover what works and what doesn't.

The steeply sloped lot meant creating a three-story facade. A new media room and covered patio replaced an old garage on the lowest level. The family room is one level up, topped by the master suite.

Overlooking the backyard, the new family room occupies the main level of the addition, which replaced an older, poorly designed addition. The space below this room was originally a tuck-under garage.

This house originally had a poorly built, contemporary addition tacked onto the back. While a buyer's first inclination might have been to accept the addition as a given and expand on it to add more space, living in the house first revealed structural problems between the addition and the original house. Add to this the style disconnect between the 1920s charm of the original and the sleek look of the addition, and there was a strong argument for razing the addition and starting over. In this instance a new, two-story wing was built on the foundation of the old addition in a style that blends with the 1920s architecture.

Details such as the gentle curve of the doorway and the battened ceiling in the family room ensure that the addition feels like "original equipment." The motif of the curve, a common embellishment in the 1920s, was used by the architect at several spots in the added space.

FLOOR PLANS ▨ addition area ▨ new structure

Main level before

Main level after

Upper level before

Upper level after

The two-story addition was the most significant change to the house, replacing a 15-year-old contemporary addition that was out of sync with the 1920s-era home. Other changes include a reconfigured kitchen and another addition that houses the library. The new master suite upstairs includes a walk-in closet carved out of an existing bedroom.

Split flagstone brings a garden-room feeling to the enclosed porch, which connects to the family room and the deck.

Living in a house reveals all sorts of subtle facets that are not immediately visible from a floor plan or even an extended walkthrough. Although renting with an option to buy would give you time to "test drive" the house, that's generally not a practical alternative. Instead, if you think a house could be your dream home with the right remodeling job, live in it for a while. Then seek the advice of an architect who can advise you on how to add on in a style that is compatible with the architecture of the existing structure.

The tub is a short walk down the hall from the vanity and miles away from the stresses of everyday life. Marble and custom detailing provide a luxurious setting in which to relax.

The new master bedroom includes a marble-top dual vanity, raised-panel cabinets, and vintage light fixtures. An antique dressing table sits in the foreground.

An arch defines a seating area in the new master bedroom. The shape can also be seen in the doors, which open to a shallow balcony.

■ Take Advantage of a Slope

A hillside can be an asset. One of the best reasons to consider a two-story addition is to make the best use of a steeply sloped lot. With proper siting you can have the extra space of a walkout basement level without overwhelming the main level with a looming addition. This trim Cape Cod, originally 1,500 square feet, almost doubled in size with a 1,300-square-foot addition on the back. But because it conforms to the slope, the two-story addition is no taller than the original house. And because the addition is slightly narrower than the original house, it is invisible from the street.

At the time of the addition, the house was a simple rectangle with a dormered half-story above and a small sunporch addition on the main level. The new 1,300-square foot addition, seen here from the side, includes a master bedroom on the main level and a media room below.

Seen from the street, the Cape Cod-style home retains all of its original charm.
The stone pillars supporting the portico match the stonework used on the addition.

A cheerfully decorated half-wall camouflages stairs leading down to the new media room without enclosing the narrow space. The breakfast table is attached to the wall with brackets to save space.

FLOOR PLAN new structure

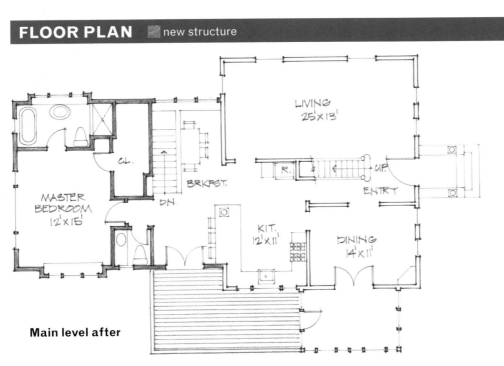

LIVING
25'x13'

CL.

BRKFST.

MASTER
BEDROOM
12'x15'

DN

ENTRY

R.

UP.

KIT.
12'x11'

DINING
14'x11'

Main level after

A key to the success of this remodel is the transitional space between the existing house and the addition. Besides helping to buffer the master bedroom from household noise, this multifunctional space includes the stairs to the lower level, two informal eating areas, and easy access to the large new deck.

Builders and designers have a variety of options for dealing with a sloping site. If the change in level is dramatic enough, full-height walls and a walkout lower level are a reasonable option. If the slope is more modest or you don't want a basement, the designer may specify a stepped foundation. This stairsteps down the slope, maintaining the proper depth for footings while requiring less excavation and concrete. In cases where the site slopes down to the house, soil can be removed to create a level zone near the house. The cut area is then stabilized with a retaining wall. Whatever options you consider, be sure to have an engineer sign off on the plans before construction begins.

The kitchen's snack bar marks the location where the original house ended. Keeping this wall open makes the kitchen feel larger. The French doors lead to the new deck.

■ Double Space with an L

The hardest part of designing a large addition is deciding where to put it.
Any one of several factors may limit expansion in a particular direction, including limited lot size, strict setback rules, or a desire not to use up the entire backyard. The problem is compounded with a two-story addition whose floor plan needs to blend with the existing traffic patterns on both levels. The 2,400-square-foot addition on this house offers a model solution to both problems: Wrap the added space around a corner of the existing house. The creative configuration minimized the impact on the yard and kept the expanded floor plan compact and efficient.

On the main level the family room opens onto a new terrace that runs the width of the house. Above, the new master bedroom features a private porch. The addition continues around the house on the right side.

Stepping back the addition at the front of the house allows the existing structure to maintain its appealing symmetry and remain the focus of the street-side view.

Built-ins keep the entertainment electronics out of sight when they're not in use and allow the elegant fireplace to serve as the family room's primary focal point. The other end of the 36-foot-long space hosts a casual dining table and doors to the adjacent patio.

The new kitchen occupies the same location as it did before the addition but was reconfigured to create an intimate relationship with the new family room. The raised snack bar limits the view into the kitchen without stifling conversation between the two rooms.

FLOOR PLANS ▨ addition area ▧ new structure

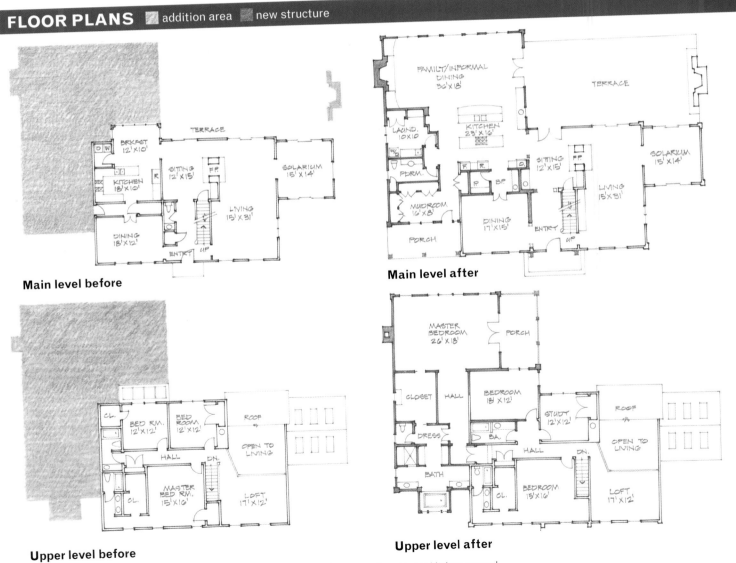

Main level before

Main level after

Upper level before

Upper level after

On the main level the addition provided a large family room for entertaining, space for a bigger kitchen, several utility rooms, and a small front porch. The high ceiling in the family room required raising the level of the master suite 2 feet above the rest of the second floor. A short flight of steps graces the entry point to the suite.

Adding an L-shape addition creates several challenges. Devising a roof plan that blends the addition with the current roof can be particularly tricky. In general it is best if the addition's roof type and slope match the existing roof, but a talented designer or architect will know when a contrasting roof style might be a more suitable option. Then there is the hassle factor. Instead of limiting mess and disruption to one side of the house, you are going to be battling dust and noise on two fronts. Although a skilled builder will do everything possible to minimize the disturbance, an extensive remodeling is by nature an imposition on the family.

HOW TO BUILD A TWO-STORY ADDITION

Building a two-story addition is similar to erecting a new two-story home. Knowledge of the parts and processes of construction will help you communicate more effectively with your designer and builder. The illustration shows the key components of a typical two-story addition.

1. Foundation. Ideally this would be the same type and depth as the home's existing foundation to avoid differential settling of old and new construction.

2. Floors. Consider manufactured joists such as the I-beams shown on the ground level or the open-web trusses shown on the second level. These prefabricated joists span longer distances than traditional joists, reducing or eliminating the need for bearing walls or support posts. Plywood subfloor is nailed to the joists, followed by finish flooring.

3. Wall framing. Walls are typically framed with 2×4s, but 2×6s can be used on exterior walls to allow for more insulation.

4. Exterior finish. Plywood or flakeboard sheathing provides structural stability to exterior walls and provides a smooth surface for attaching weatherization fabric and siding. Windows can be installed once sheathing is in place.

5. Interior finish. Gypsum wallboard is applied to interior surfaces following installation of plumbing, wiring, and insulation.

6. Roof. Most builders opt for trusses rather than traditional hand-framing. Costs are lower and the quality is high, although most truss designs do not provide attic space. Sheathing, roofing paper, and shingles complete the roof.

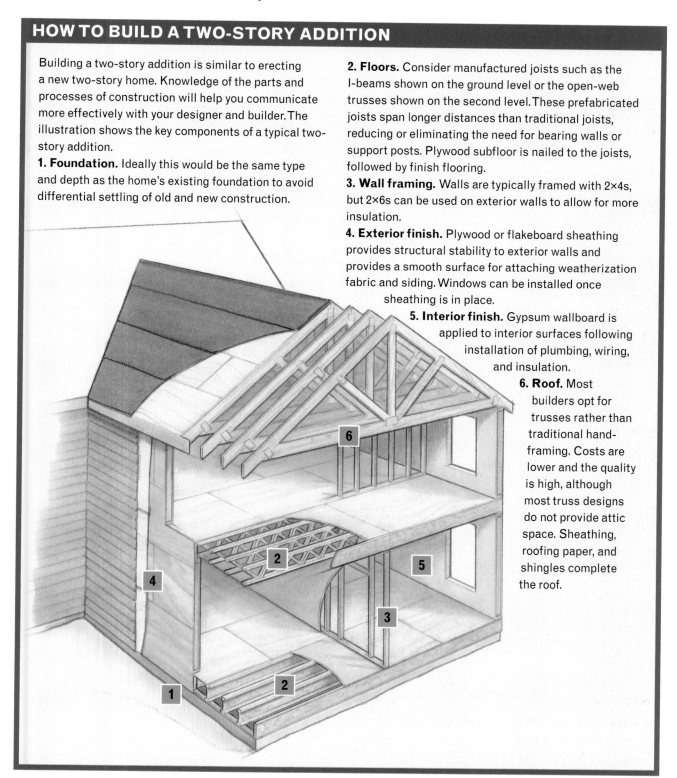

Another drawback to an L-shape addition is cost. An L-shape costs more to build than a rectangle of the same area because it requires more exterior wall area, a more extensive foundation, and more work on the exterior walls of the existing house.

Despite these challenges, a wraparound addition may be the only way to dramatically increase the size of a home. If moving is out of the question, the extra cost may well be worth it.

Located directly above the family room, the new master bedroom is linked to dressing and bathing areas by a wide hallway. The vaulted ceiling gives this large room an elegant feeling.

The spa tub in the master suite sits in a small bumpout in the narrow section of the addition. Both the tub surround and the floor are clad in tumbled-marble tiles.

The master bedroom porch offers a tranquil place to relax and enjoy the view.

Two-story additions are a good way to substantially increase the size of a home if you can't add the equivalent amount of space on one level. This arises in areas where setbacks prevent sprawling additions or on sites where the terrain is not well-suited to a large foundation.

Another reason to go the two-story route: the desire to add bedroom space upstairs and living areas on the main level. You could achieve this with separate additions but probably at a higher cost.

Configurations. Often a two-story addition is grafted onto the existing home with both new and old space sharing a common wall. This approach allows excellent integration of the new floor space but also requires living with lots of mess during construction. The intrusions are greatest when the original house wall is removed or reframed to join the old and new rooms. Work with your contractor to devise strategies for containing the worst of the mess and minimizing the time you'll be exposed.

Another design approach is to build the addition as a separate tower that is linked to the existing house via short passageways on one or both levels. This approach limits demolition work and the disruption it causes. Costs can also be lower because there's no need to tear into walls containing electric lines, plumbing pipes, venting stacks, and chimneys. Moving any of these utilities is expensive.

Utilities. Unless an addition is quite small relative to the existing house, you will almost certainly

Visitors would have a hard time believing that the dormered, two-story addition to this house was built in a factory, then trucked to the site in sections.

Additions

need to upgrade the heating and cooling system or install separate systems in the addition. Minor upgrades to electrical and plumbing systems may also be needed if they have not been modernized. See page 216 for specific advice about utilities for additions.

Building method. Most two-story additions are built piece by piece on the site, using the same materials and techniques used in traditional home building. The advantage of stick-building is that contractors are familiar with the process and can make adjustments (for a cost) at almost any stage of construction.

An alternative approach is modular construction. With this approach, the addition is built in a factory (in one or more sections), then trucked to the site, placed on a new foundation, and married to the existing structure, usually by a local general contractor. Because the addition is roughly 80 percent complete when it arrives on your lot, the modular approach is much less disruptive. Construction time and cost are usually lower than conventionally built additions—but not always. Modular construction requires precise measurements of your home to ensure a good fit. Hire a contractor with experience with your type of project. As with any addition, have an engineer review the plans to ensure that the existing structure is able to handle the loads imposed by the addition.

Surviving a Major Remodeling

A two-story addition may turn your household upside down for months.

Not all parts of a two-story addition need to be enclosed. This rear-facing add-on features a screen porch and kitchen on the lower level and a master suite above.

Here are some tips to get through it:

Make contingency plans. If you can't abandon ship during the remodeling, rearrange rooms before work begins. Set up a temporary cooking area in another room if your kitchen will be out of commission.

Confine the mess. Hang tarps in doorways to seal off rooms where remodeling is under way. Some dust will escape the work zone, so cover sensitive equipment or valuable furnishings throughout the house. Also keep expensive telephones out of the remodeling area. Have waste materials hauled frequently.

Avoid fumes. Pin down the periods when glues, finishes, or other odorous materials will be used. Make certain the house will be well-ventilated when smells are at their peak.

Communicate. Discuss the project frequently with your contractor so you are prepared for changes to the schedule or order of construction.

Contract Pointers

The larger your remodeling project, the more critical the contract with your builder becomes. In addition to reviewing any contract with

A single-level addition like this clapboard-sided family room can easily be upgraded to provide two stories of utility by addng a deck and railing above the flat roof.

Additions

your lawyer, watch for these basic elements:

Project description. A detailed list of what the contractor will and will not do.

Time table. The project's start date, milestone dates, and completion date and a contingency clause for events (like bad weather) or hidden conditions (like termites in the subfloor) that may mean delays or extra expense.

Product specifications. A detailed list of products to be used, including brands and model numbers. Don't let the contractor specify "or an item of comparable quality." Also note products you will buy and who will install them.

Price and payment schedule. Total price, itemized, along with payment amounts and due dates. A portion of the cost (25 to 33 percent) should be due only after the project is approved by you and the local building department and the builder can produce lien releases from all subcontractors.

Warranties. Terms of product and workmanship warranties and the names and addresses of the parties responsible for fulfilling them.

Change orders. Explanations of how amendments to the contract will

Thanks to a double lot, finding space for this addition (to the left of the entry) was simple. The 2,000-square-foot add-on echoes the gambrel roof of the original home.

be handled. All changes, no matter how small, should be recorded as a modification of the original contract.

Making It

Turning dreams into reality is an exciting, if challenging, task. The information in this chapter will help you move beyond the "just looking" phase into the serious work of building an addition. Some of the ideas and information here should serve as a reality check that will prevent an expensive mistake. But most of the advice is designed to make the transition from planning to completion as smooth as possible. By following this advice—and your heart—you will likely enjoy a successful, even life-changing, experience.

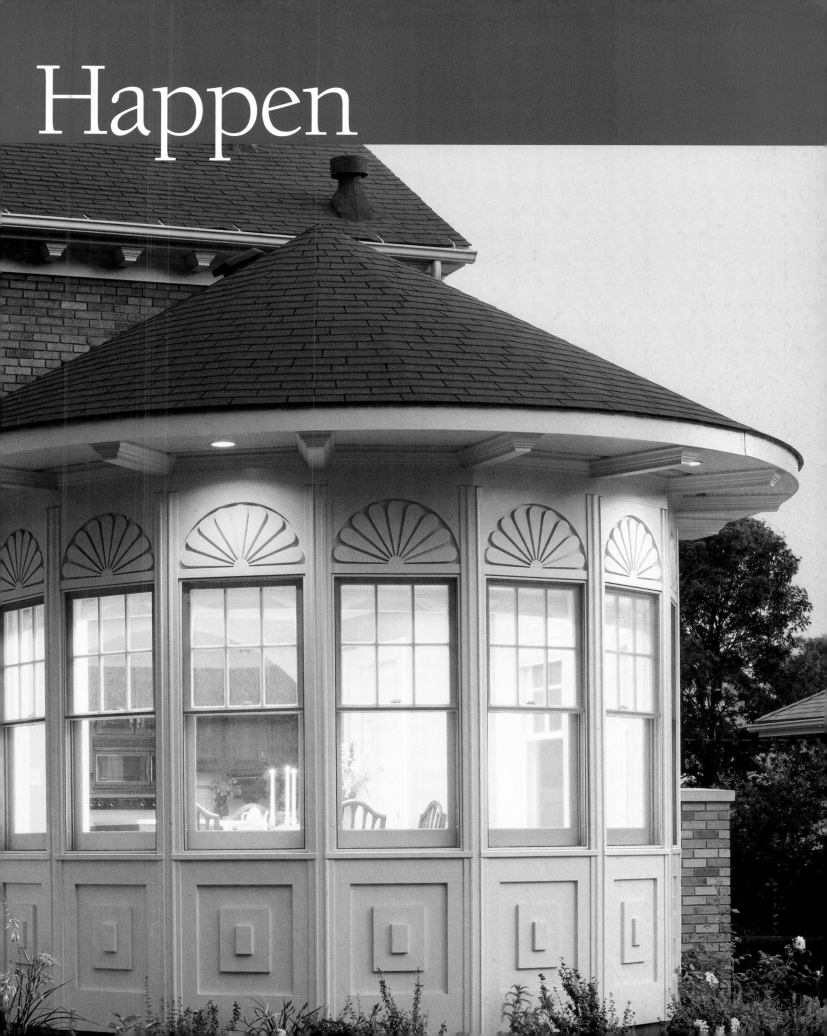

Happen

■ Why an Addition?

Why build an addition? There's really only one good answer: because you have the money and it will make you the happiest person on earth. Of course this presumes honesty on both counts. An addition will likely cost more than you expect, so ready access to funds—either through loans or cash—is critical. The other criterion, happiness, may be the only thing that gets you through weeks or months of negotiation, compromise, mess, and complete and total inconvenience.

Question 2: What sort of addition should you build? Again there's only one "best" answer: one that makes a house as good as or a little better than the other houses in the neighborhood. You don't want to find yourself owing more to the bank than you could get from a sale. Of course if your enjoyment of the addition matters more to you than recouping your investment, go ahead and add a $150,000 kitchen to your $100,000 bungalow. Just don't say you weren't warned.

DEFINING YOUR DESIRES

To help guide planning and decision making, take the time to answer some key questions:

• What do you like most about your house? What do you like least?
• Which rooms are too small?
• Are you satisfied with the size, location, and features of your kitchen?
• Does your home's layout allow you to entertain comfortably?
• Do you have adequate bedroom space for each family member?
• Is there a comfortable space for everyday dining?
• Do you long for a room that connects well to outdoor living areas?
• Does your master bedroom have enough closet space and comfort features?
• Do you have separate places for noisy activities and quiet pursuits?

Sunrooms are common additions because they support a casual lifestyle and add flexible living space.

■ Your Home's First Report Card

First things first. Before progressing too far on your remodeling plans, you'll need an honest assessment of your home's present condition. An addition creates stresses that may overwhelm the existing structure. A new second story may require beefing up the foundation. And even a small sunroom addition may overwhelm heating and cooling systems already operating at the edge of capacity.

Depending on the size and complexity of your project, you'll need to hire a home inspector or consulting engineer. Here are the areas you should expect to be covered in the report:

Roof. Is the underlying framework in good condition? Are shingles or other roofing materials in good shape? Ensure that chimneys and vents are sound.

Exterior walls. Are all walls straight and even? Are the siding and trim in good shape? Are windows and doors weathersealed and in good operating condition? Is the paint in good shape?

Foundation. Are there cracks or loose materials? Are there any signs of water leakage or insect damage? Is there evidence of uneven settling? Is the foundation capable of supporting the extra weight of an addition?

Interiors. Are walls, floors, and ceilings level, square, and solid? Are there signs of water leaks or uneven settling (such as cracks around doors or windows)?

Plumbing. Are all fixtures in good working condition? Is there any evidence of leaks? Are water pressure and hot water supply adequate? Do drains and vents operate properly? Is the system up to current codes?

Electrical service. Is there adequate capacity in the system to handle added demands? Are wires, outlets, switches, and fixtures in good condition? Does the system meet current code requirements?

Heating, cooling, and ventilation. Is the mechanical equipment in good condition? Does the system have the capacity to serve added space?

Before advancing your addition's plans, have your home inspected from footings to roof peak and correct any shortcomings or problems you find.

■ Consider Your Options

Additions come in many styles, each with its own advantages and disadvantages. Before you commit to your ultimate dream addition, consider whether a less ambitious project might actually serve your needs better. Here's a rundown of the addition types to consider:

A bumpout is often a good option for expanding a room at the front of the house.

Dormers are an inexpensive way to create livable space in an attic.

Bay windows, bumpouts, and dormers. These modest add-ons are a great way to loosen tight spaces within a tight budget or to bring light into dark spaces. All three can be sized to handle a particular feature, such as a fireplace, built-in bed, or dinette table. In most cases no additional foundation is required, which keeps the cost low and sidesteps setback restrictions that might limit expansion of your home. Bay windows and small bumpouts are the simplest to install. Consider hiring a designer or an architect for larger bumpouts and dormers, which may look out of place on your home unless blended skillfully with the existing structure.

Room additions. If your home is lacking a particular type of space, such as a family room, sunroom, or dining room, a single-room addition may be the way to go. The key to a successful room addition is blending old and new into an attractive and useful whole. An architect or skilled designer

can help match materials and proportions on the outside and ensure that the new room fits naturally into the home's floor plan. Save money by opting for a builder's "package"—combining design, materials, and construction—but consider having an independent expert evaluate the quality of the design and materials before signing a contract.

Second-story additions. No remodeling project is more challenging than adding an upper level to a house. Still there are times when you can't build out, and building up is your only option. Even before design work begins, you'll need to have a structural engineer evaluate your home's foundation and walls to determine whether they'll need shoring up—an

This room addition connects to the corner of the house to maximize window area.

expensive undertaking. Construction may be somewhat easier if you already have a partial upper level. Otherwise you will have to find space on the lower level for a stairway.

Two-story additions. Consider this option if you need extra space but because of logistical or zoning restrictions you can't add it all to one level. You'll certainly need a designer or architect to evaluate the design of the addition and the best way to integrate the floor plans on each level. Though an expensive approach, a two-story addition requires less foundation and roofing than a similar-size single-story add-on, so the cost may be a bit lower. Except for very small additions, you'll likely need to add separate heating and cooling equipment to avoid overtaxing your current system.

Wing additions. Adding multiple rooms in a single stroke allows you to reshape the very essence of your house. For example, you might combine a kitchen, great-room, and home theater to create the ideal setup for entertaining. Or you could add a bedroom wing for the kids' rooms so that you can expand the master suite far beyond its current cramped quarters. Wing additions make the most economic sense for a house that is woefully underbuilt for the neighborhood. Just be sure that your plans square with local building and zoning requirements.

To avoid changing the horizontal character of the original house, this second-story addition tops just a portion of the lower level.

■ Blending Old and New

The ability to create a beautiful blend of old and new is what makes designers and architects so valuable to an addition project. Design pros typically focus on three elements to achieve this blending: the materials (siding, trim, windows, and so on), roof type and pitch, and proportion. The three illustrations on this page illuminate how those elements can be harmonized to produce an attractive appearance.

CREATING VINTAGE CHARACTER

One of the challenges of adding onto an older home is finding materials, fixtures, and trimwork that match the originals. While you can't always find an exact match, selecting items that hark back to the same era can give good results, even if those items were manufactured last week using modern materials. If large home centers or local salvage yards don't offer what you need, check out these resources:
* Restoration Hardware: renovation superstore (restorationhardware.com)
* Renovator's Supply: bath fixtures (rensup.com)
* Classic Details: architectural details (classicdetails .com)
* E.R. Butler & Co.: hardware (erbutler.com)

* Secondhand Rose: wall coverings (secondhandrose .com)
* Starke Millwork: molding and trim (starkemillwork .com)
* Studio Steel: light fixtures (studiosteel.com)
* YesterYear's Vintage Doors: doors and accents (vintagedoors.com)

Better. Definitely an improvement. The board siding has been replaced by stucco, and the angles of the roof match the original gable. The addition is still out of proportion to the house, however, and the contemporary freeform windows are out of character for this vintage home.

Bad. This attempt at a second-story addition does everything wrong. The board siding is a departure from the stucco finish on the original house, and the tiny windows are at odds with the larger originals. Similarly, the addition's roof matches neither the style of the original nor its generous overhangs. Finally, the addition's proportions are awkward—notice how it ends abruptly about two-thirds of the way across the gabled section on the main level.

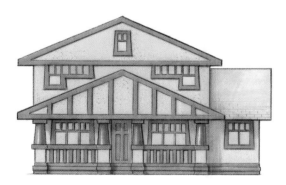

Best. This example pulls it all together. The siding and rooflines match the original, and the addition ends at a natural stopping point along the facade. Although not an exact match, the addition's windows maintain the basic feel of the original units. Most observers would have a tough time identifying new and old in this view.

■ Assembling Your Team

For most people, building an addition requires hiring and working with experts. Here are the professionals you will want to consider hiring:

Architect. An architect with experience in home remodeling projects can suggest creative solutions to difficult problems and will ensure that you are getting the most for your budget. The detailed drawings that your architect creates will allow the contractor to work efficiently and without a lot of guesswork. The commission for complete design services generally starts at 10 to 15 percent of the cost of the project, but many architects will consider hourly charges for limited consulting responsibilities.

Home designer. Nonlicensed designers may lack professional credentials, but they can still have the experience and talent needed to turn your ideas into a workable set of plans. Especially for smaller projects, you may have an easier time finding a designer than an architect to take on the job. A portfolio brimming with successful projects is a good indication of a designer's effectiveness.

Design/build firm. Combine a design team with a general contractor and you have a one-stop shop for your project. Because the two teams are experienced at working together, even difficult projects are likely to go smoothly.

Kitchen and/or bath designer. Choose a specialized designer particularly if you want to incorporate cutting-edge products and the latest trends into your remodel. For an extra measure of confidence, look for designers certified by the National Kitchen and Bath Association.

Contractor. A general contractor has overall responsibility for the construction of your addition. He or she hires the subcontractors for framing, roofing, foundation work, trim installation, and so on. Among the general contractor's most critical roles is scheduling the subcontractors at precisely the right time to keep the project moving efficiently.

Hiring the right person. Invest time and energy finding the right people. That means soliciting recommendations from friends and acquaintances, interviewing multiple candidates, looking into customer and business references, and checking with the Better Business Bureau.

Even if you choose to have a builder or designer plan your addition, it will be worthwhile to have an architect review the plans.

Going Green and Healthy

You can save on utility bills, help keep your family healthy, and reduce your home's impact on the environment by making smart choices when building your addition. Be on the lookout for products that produce fewer toxic emissions or make better use of energy. Here are some examples:

Building materials. Work with your designer and contractor to locate and use materials that are salvaged, recycled, or locally produced. Choose water-base finishes, which release few toxic gases, and building materials made without formaldehyde and other toxic chemicals. Specify carpeting and installation materials that are CRI (Carpet and Rug Institute) Green Label Plus-certified for low emissions of undesirable chemicals. When selecting wood flooring, ask about FCS (Forest Stewardship Council) certification, which indicates that the wood was produced in an environmentally responsible manner.

Windows, appliances, and heating and cooling equipment. Where possible, specify products that carry an Energy Star label. This certification identifies products that are substantially more energy-efficient than the average for that category.

Lighting. About 10 percent of the average home's electric bill goes toward lighting. Choosing the most energy-efficient fixtures and bulbs can produce dramatic savings. Compact fluorescent bulbs use only one-third as much energy as incandescent bulbs and last 10 times longer. Light fixtures that carry the Energy Star label distribute light more effectively than typical fixtures.

Natural heating and cooling. In northern regions, outfit your addition with south-facing windows to capture the winter sun's warmth. In the South orient windows to the north to reduce heat gain in summer. In all locations site your addition to capture cooling breezes and plant deciduous trees (those that lose their leaves in the fall) to provide shade in summer and sunshine in winter.

Insulation and weatherization. Insulate walls, ceilings, foundations, and floors over crawlspaces to as high a level as feasible. Ask your designer or builder to specify products and building techniques that minimize unwanted leakage of conditioned air to the outside.

For maximum energy efficiency choose Energy Star-rated fixtures and outfit them with compact fluorescent bulbs.

■ Design for All

Universal design is a set of standards and principles that are used to create spaces that everyone can use and enjoy regardless of age or ability. Although it is associated with wheelchair access, universal design is really a much broader concept. It is particularly important to older homeowners who desire to remain in their homes as long as possible.

When planning an addition, consider these elements of universal design:

- Reduce changes in level. As much as practical, plan for single-level living. Even a single step can create a barrier to a person with mobility problems.
- Think "easy to operate." Choose products that require less effort to use. Levers are easier to use than the typical doorknob. And appliances with large, easy-to-read settings are easier on those with less than 20/20 vision.
- Maintain clearances. Wide hallways and door openings make it easier for people maneuvering wheelchairs, walkers, and the like.
- Put safety first. Install grab bars in bathrooms and handrails beside all staircases. Build outdoor walks

Universal design can be beautiful. The cabinets below this cooktop open to reveal space for a wheelchair.

Specialized appliances make it easier to put universal design principles into action. This side-opening wall oven is mounted at a height that cuts down on reaching up and bending over.

with textured, nonskid surfaces. Avoid flooring that is slippery when wet in areas such as entries and mudrooms.

- Keep it bright. Provide plenty of light at entries, in hallways and closets, and on stairs.
- Provide accessible storage. Install pullout trays, lazy Susans, baskets, raised shoe racks, and similar convenience features. Add a second clothes rod at a lower level to double hanging storage and put frequently used items on the lower rod.
- Keep things in reach. Install light switches and thermostats a little lower to make them easier for a sitting person to reach.
- Give kitchens and baths special treatment. Because of the complex nature of these rooms and the many building codes that impact them, it makes sense to hire professional help to create universally accessible spaces. An architect, designer, or local Easter Seals chapter can put you in touch with local resources.

Selecting Your Materials

The finish materials you select for your addition affect more than its appearance. In particular, your choices of flooring, siding, and roofing influence project costs, its durability, and the amount of time spent on maintenance.

Flooring	Strengths	Weaknesses
Carpeting	Comfortable; wide color choice	Prone to stains and traffic wear
Laminate	Durable and easy to install; many colors/patterns; low maintenance	Damage can be hard to repair.
Resilient	Waterproof; wide range of colors and patterns; relatively low cost	Prone to damage; requires periodic replacement.
Tile/stone	Long lifespan; unique looks	Can feel cold; needs regular sealing
Solid wood	Warm; many colors and species; long-lasting; low maintenance; engineered wood offers the look of solid wood at a lower cost.	Subject to moisture damage; requires occasional refinishing; prefinished products offer fewer color/species options.

Siding	Strengths	Weaknesses
Wood board and shingle	Easy to install; wide variety of looks, can be painted or stained	Requires periodic repainting; subject to insect and water damage
Vinyl and aluminum	Low maintenance; long lifespan; stable color; available in several quality grades	Low-cost types offer limited color range and trim options; inexpensive vinyl may sag in high heat.
Hardboard	Low cost and easy to install	Requires repainting; limited lifespan
Brick or stone	Unique looks; wide range of colors and styles; long lifespan	Requires special construction to support weight; expensive
Fiber-cement	Long lifespan; not subject to moisture or insect damage	Expensive; requires periodic repainting

Roofing	Strengths	Weaknesses
Asphalt and composition	Durable, inexpensive, and easy to install; dimensional products offer the look of wood shakes.	Subject to weather damage in extreme conditions; not as distinctive looking as other roofing materials
Shakes and shingles	Long lifespan; unique look	Expensive
Tile	Very long lifespan; unique look	Requires extra roof support
Metal	Durable and long-lasting; available in many looks and colors	Expensive

■ Windows

The design of an addition will dictate the size and type of windows you include, but there are other choices to make too. These options fall into three categories:

Material. Window frames can be made from wood, vinyl, or aluminum. Wood is the traditional material, a good insulator, and paintable. To reduce maintenance, wood frames can be faced with aluminum or vinyl. Today's vinyl windows are much improved over older versions and continue to be less expensive and lower maintenance than wood. Aluminum is not a good insulator, so windows made from this material are best suited to warm climates.

Energy efficiency. You'll save on heating and cooling costs and have a more comfortable house if you buy windows with top energy-efficiency ratings. Almost all windows are made with insulating double-pane glass; better units have argon or other gas in the space to further improve efficiency. Low-E glass sports a thin metallic coating that keeps heat outside in summer and inside in winter. When comparing windows, the higher the R rating, the better.

Convenience features. Among the best options: tilt-in sashes that make cleaning easy; dust-free between-the-glass shades and blinds; art glass inserts for a vintage look; and "invisible" insect screens.

Windows are a huge factor in heating and cooling bills. You will get a good return on an investment in the most energy-efficient units.

Heating, Cooling, Plumbing, and Electricity

If your home's systems are more than 25 years old, you may be facing large bills for upgrades to service an addition. Be sure to review all your options with your architect or contractor early in the planning process. Here are some considerations to weigh.

ELECTRICAL SYSTEMS

Adding capacity to an existing system is neither difficult nor particularly expensive. Your primary job during the planning process is anticipating your needs for outlets, switches, and light fixtures. Give these items a lot of thought early on, because including them during construction is inexpensive compared to the cost of adding them later. Study your new floor plan and think about the way your family lives. Are you satisfied with the way the home is presently wired? Are outlets at the right spots for small appliances? Might you want to add a home theater, security system, or sophisticated sound system later?

PLUMBING SYSTEMS

In additions that require new plumbing, try to maneuver plans to limit trunk lines off the main plumbing pipes. If you are plumbing a laundry, can it share a plumbing wall with the kitchen? Bathrooms placed back to back can also share plumbing services.

HEATING AND AIR-CONDITIONING (HVAC)

Maintaining the comfort level of your addition requires adequate heating and cooling. It's wise to bring in professionals to determine if your equipment can handle the extra space or if you will need additional equipment. If you have to purchase new equipment, here are choices you will face:

Forced-air systems. These systems heat or cool air at a central location using gas (natural or propane), oil, or electricity, then circulate the conditioned air throughout the house using fans. If the system is more than 25 years old, chances are it is nearing the end of its life and should be replaced. Systems installed before 1992 are likely to be energy wasters. Installing new, high-efficiency models can reduce your heating and cooling bills, but you'll want to weigh these savings against the initial cost of installation. Rather than replace both a furnace and central air-conditioner, you could install a heat pump, a device that combines both functions; heat pumps make the most sense in relatively mild climates. A good contractor or architect can help you run the numbers on all of your options.

Hot-water systems. In this case water is heated in a boiler, then piped to radiators throughout the house. Again the decision to replace boils down to age and energy efficiency. Switching to a forced-

It makes sense to consider possible future enhancements when planning the wiring for your addition.

Save on plumbing costs by clustering fixtures, either on one level or stacked on multiple levels.

The older your heating and cooling systems are, the more sense it makes to upgrade when you add on.

air system is feasible, but adding ductwork may be costly. One other consideration: With a hot-water system you'll need a separate system to handle air-conditioning.

Electrical radiant systems. Using electrically warmed wires, either in baseboard heaters or under the floor, is a relatively expensive way to heat a home but easy to install and expand. This option is best for small additions or those in mild climates.

Geothermal systems. In winter a geothermal system captures heat below the frost line, where temperatures remain about 55°F year-round. In summer the system releases heat to the same

ground. Geothermal systems are very inexpensive to operate but can be very expensive to install. Again, your contractor can help you weigh the costs and payback.

Room units. For a single-room addition, installing a separate heating and cooling system may be the best option. Wallmount furnaces fueled by electricity, propane, or natural gas are available in a variety of sizes. And single-room air-conditioners, either wallmount or window-mounted, are easy to install. The downside to single-room heating and cooling is that it may hurt your home's resale value.

Finding the Money

For most remodelers the money to fund their projects comes from some combination of three sources, each with its own advantages.

Cash. A reasonable option for relatively small projects, paying cash offers the fewest hassles of any funding source. But even if you have adequate funds in the bank, paying cash does have some drawbacks. Financing your project with a tax-deductible loan and putting your cash into an interest-bearing account might actually cost you less in the long run.

Unsecured loans. If you are willing to pay relatively (or extremely) high interest rates, lenders and credit card companies are a relatively hassle-free source of funds. Another drawback is the lack of deductibility of interest payments. An unsecured loan may be your only borrowing option if you have little or no equity in your home.

Secured loans. The most common form of financing for large remodeling projects is a loan secured by the value of your home. These sources of funds offer lower interest rates than unsecured loans and offer the bonus of a tax deduction for interest paid. Home equity loans (or second mortgages) provide a fixed amount paid off in equal monthly installments. Home equity lines of credit let you borrow the money as you need it and pay it off over time, typically at an interest rate that varies. Cash-out refinancing allows you to borrow enough to pay off your first mortgage and pay for the remodeling.

Other options. The Federal Housing Administration (FHA) offers two special home improvement programs aimed at low- to moderate-income remodelers. The Title I loan lets you borrow up to $25,000 for a single-family dwelling at a fixed rate. The Section 203(k) loan is an option if you purchase a fixer-upper; you can receive a single, long-term, fixed- or adjustable-rate loan for the purchase and the rehabilitation of a property. For more details on these programs, visit www.hud.gov.

You may also be able to borrow against a 401(k) or 403(b) retirement plan or a whole life insurance policy. While the interest rate may be lower than a typical bank rate, these options also put your future security at risk. Proceed with caution.

SIX WAYS TO CUT YOUR REMODELING COSTS
- Hire a design professional.
- Hire a general contractor.
- Purchase materials on sale.
- Don't make changes after construction begins.
- Inspect the work often to catch problems early.
- Shop for the lowest cost financing.

Salvage yards are an excellent source of reasonably priced materials and fixtures, but be sure your builder is comfortable working with your purchases.

■ The Construction Process

Once you have a design in hand and a realistic budget set, remodeling moves from the dreaming phase to the doing stage. Here's what to expect:

PRECONSTRUCTION

- Review the design with your contractor for feasibility and improvements.
- Work with your contractor to set a timeline for selecting materials and products.
- Ask the contractor to provide a construction schedule, apply for permits, and select subcontractors.
- Tour your house with the key players—job-site supervisors, key subcontractors, designers, for example—to review the job in detail.
- Set ground rules on matters like access to the house, parking, and times of day when construction is permitted.
- Select a primary contact (usually the job-site supervisor) and agree on a system for trading comments.
- If appropriate, set up a mini kitchen in another part of the house.

DEMOLITION

- Your room or house gets the treatment from the wrecking crew.
- Ensure that plastic sheeting seals the demolition area from the rest of the house.

CONSTRUCTION

- The crew prepares the foundation; frames the walls, floors, and roof; and installs windows.
- The plumbing is roughed in; electric, phone, and cable lines are run; and conduits for HVAC systems are installed.
- Insulation, drywall, and floor underlayments are installed.
- The house is roofed and sided.
- The crew finishes walls and ceilings; installs cabinets, counters, and trim; and hooks up appliances and light fixtures.
- Finish flooring is installed and plumbing and electrical systems are completed.

FOLLOW-UP

- Tour the remodeled space with your contractor, itemizing any details that need to be finished or corrected.
- Complete a final inspection with the contractor, checking off the items from your preliminary walkthrough.
- Over a few months' time, ensure that everything works properly and watch for drywall cracks or nail pops. Call the contractor for any follow-up repairs.

Insist on a daily meeting with your contractor or jobsite supervisor to review progress and resolve problems.

■ Glossary

Awning window A top-hinged window that swings out from the bottom.

Baseboard Interior trim that covers the joint between the wall and the floor.

Beam A horizontal framing member that carries the weight of a wall, roof, or floor.

Bearing wall A wall that supports a floor, roof, or another wall above it.

Building codes Local regulations that control the construction of buildings for safety and public health. These regulations are often modeled on national codes created by professional organizations.

Building inspector A local government worker who ensures that buildings are constructed according to the building codes.

Building permit A notice stating that a construction project plan has been reviewed and approved by a local building department.

Bumpout A section of a building that extends out from the foundation beneath it.

Casement window A window that is hinged on one side and opens like a door.

Casing Decorative trim used around doors and windows to cover gaps or rough framing.

Cladding Any material—such as siding, brick, or stone—attached to the exterior of a structure for protection against the weather.

Deconstruction The careful removal of existing fixtures (such as kitchen cabinets) prior to remodeling or renovation so they can be reused elsewhere.

Double-hung window A window with two sashes that slide up or down in tracks.

Drywall Interior wallcovering that is applied in large sheets or panels. Also known as wallboard.

Ductwork Large, hollow tubes that carry air between the heating or cooling system and rooms in a house.

Engineered material A building material created by combining two or more materials. Examples include laminated beams, particleboard, and synthetic stone.

Flashing Sheet metal or other material used in roof and wall construction to direct water away from openings in walls or roofs, such as around chimneys, above windows, or around skylights.

Footing The enlarged base of a foundation wall or column that supports the weight of the house.

Foundation The base that supports a building or other structure.

Framing The process of building the wood or metal framework of walls, floors, ceilings, and roofs.

Frost line The maximum depth to which ground freezes in a specific location.

General contractor The person or company hired to oversee a building project. The "general" hires, supervises, and pays subcontractors.

Green construction A set of principles designed to produce structures with less impact on the environment through the use of energy-saving technology, low-toxicity materials, and renewable resources.

Header A structural element that supports the weight of a structure above a window or door.

House wrap Woven synthetic sheeting applied over sheathing that allows moisture but not air to pass into or out of the house. Used to improve energy efficiency.

HVAC Heating, ventilating, and air-conditioning system.

Insulation Material used to reduce heat loss in winter or heat gain in summer. Available in many forms, including fiberglass batting or blankets, rigid foam boards, and loose-fill cellulose. The higher the R-value, the more effective the insulation.

Joist A horizontal framing member that supports a floor or ceiling.

Laminate A hard, durable plastic veneer used as a finished surface on counters, cabinets, and flooring.

Molding Decorative trim used to embellish a wall, door, or window; often used to cover a gap where two materials meet.

Plate The horizontal member nailed to the top (the top plate) or bottom (bottom plate) of a stud wall.

Rafter The main supporting member of a roof.

Rebar A steel rod cast into concrete to strengthen it.

Riser The vertical portion of a stairway above the treads.

Rough-in The installation of pipes, wires, ducts, and other mechanical systems within unfinished walls, floors, and ceilings.

Sash The frame that holds the glass panes in a window.

Setback The minimum distance allowed between a property line and a build. Setbacks are set by local building codes.

Sheathing A layer of plywood or similar material applied to the exterior side of a wall or roof to provide strength and a base for attaching finish materials.

Sill A horizontal member that rests on the foundation and supports the floor joists. Also the bottom of a window or door frame.

Stringer A diagonal support structure under a staircase.

Stud framing A building system of lightweight, closely spaced vertical members (studs) joined by horizontal members (plates) that forms the structure of most of the walls in a house.

Subfloor The structural base of a floor over which the finished floor is installed. The most common subfloor materials are plywood, wood, and concrete.

Timber framing A building system that uses heavy, widely spaced wooden members to construct walls. The structural members are left exposed for decorative effect. Also called post-and-beam framing.

Tread The step portion of a staircase.

Truss A framework of wood or metal that is designed to be lightweight but strong. Most commonly used to build roofs, trusses can also be used as floor and ceiling joists.

Vapor barrier Material or coating that prevents the migration of water vapor through a wall.

■ Index

Transform your home
into the living space you've always wanted

Better Homes and Gardens
KITCHEN
IDEA FILE
Ranges • Refrigerators • Cabinets • Lighting

IDEAS & HOW-TO
Trimwork
Better Homes
Molding • Mantels • Built-Ins • Wa

Better Homes and Gardens
color
scheme
made

decorative
pair
techniques & ideas

Better Homes and Gardens
ALL NEW EDITION
• Hundreds of idea-filled photos
• Quick and easy projects
• Before & after makeovers
• Dozens of styles
new
decorating
book
Better Homes

Imagine living in a space customized for you, by you. These great titles will help make your dreams come true with style ideas, design tips and step-by-step instructions.

Meredith®
BOOKS